The Scarecrow Author Bibliographies

1. John Steinbeck (Tetsumaro Hayashi). 1973.
2. Joseph Conrad (Theodore G. Ehrsam). 1969.
3. Arthur Miller (Tetsumaro Hayashi). 2d ed.   due 1976.
4. Katherine Anne Porter (Waldrip & Bauer).   1969.
5. Philip Freneau (Philip M. Marsh).   1970.
6. Robert Greene (Tetsumaro Hayashi).   1971.
7. Benjamin Disraeli (R. W. Stewart).   1972.
8. John Berryman (Richard W. Kelly).   1972.
9. William Dean Howells (Vito J. Brenni).   1973.
10. Jean Anouilh (Kathleen W. Kelly).   1973.
11. E. M. Forster (Alfred Borrello).   1973.
12. The Marquis de Sade (E. Pierre Chanover).   1973.
13. Alain Robbe-Grillet (Dale W. Frazier).   1973.
14. Northrop Frye (Robert D. Denham).   1974.
15. Federico García Lorca (Laurenti & Siracusa).   1974.
16. Ben Jonson (Brock & Welsh).   1974.
17. Four French Dramatists: Eugène Brieux, Francois de Curel, Emile Fabre, Paul Hervieu (Edmund F. Santa Vicca).   1974.
18. Ralph Waldo Ellison (Jacqueline Covo).   1974.
19. Philip Roth (Bernard F. Rodgers, Jr.).   1974.
20. Norman Mailer (Laura Adams).   1974.
21. Sir John Betjeman (Margaret Stapleton).   1974.
22. Elie Wiesel (Molly Abramowitz).   1974.
23. Paul Laurence Dunbar (Eugene W. Metcalf, Jr.).   1975.
24. Henry James (Beatrice Ricks).   1975.
25. Robert Frost (Lentricchia & Lentricchia).   1976.
26. Sherwood Anderson (Douglas G. Rogers).   1976.
27. Iris Murdoch and Muriel Spark (Tominaga and Schneider-meyer).   1976.
28. John Ruskin (Kirk H. Beetz).   1976.
29. Georges Simenon (Trudee Young).   1976.
30. George Gordon, Lord Byron (Oscar Jose Santucho).   1976.
31. John Barth (Richard Vine).   1977.
32. John Hawkes (Carol A. Hryciw).   1977.
33. William Everson (Bartlett & Campo).   1977.

JOHN HAWKES:

An Annotated Bibliography

by

CAROL A. HRYCIW

With Four Introductions

by

JOHN HAWKES

The Scarecrow Press, Inc.

Metuchen, N.J.   1977

Library of Congress Cataloging in Publication Data

Hryciw, Carol A   1946-
    John Hawkes.

    (The Scarecrow author bibliographies ; no. 32)
    Includes indexes.
    1.   Hawkes, John, 1925-   --Bibliography.
Z8392. 5. H79   [PS3558. A82]   016. 813'5'4   77-700
ISBN 0-8108-1024-7

Dedicated to the memory of my parents

CONTENTS

FOUR INTRODUCTIONS

John Hawkes

It was my special pleasure to introduce Anaïs Nin at
her Harvard Advocate reading in 1960; Albert J. Guerard at
his reading at Harvard in 1961 (when Guerard announced his
resignation from Harvard in order to accept the Albert Leon
Guerard Professorship at Stanford); John Barth at his reading
which he gave as part of his visit to the Voice Project at
Stanford in 1966; and Bernard Malamud when he read at
Brown in 1971. The texts of these introductions follow.

Anaïs Nin (Harvard, 1960)

The novels of Anaïs Nin, like those of Proust, com-
prise in fact a single extended novel entitled Cities of the Interior. During the past year Miss Nin published the first
volume of this work, a volume that contains five of her novels
--Ladders to Fire, Children of the Albatross, Four Chambered
Heart, A Spy in the House of Love and Solar Barque. Recently I have been rereading some of Anaïs Nin's "dramas of
the unconscious," as she has called them, and I find, uncom-
fortably, that I have literally begun to dream at night the
dreams dreamed by Lillian, one of the central figures of
Cities of the Interior. Shocking as it may be, perhaps we
should expect this kind of disquieting and pleasurable effect
from the work of a writer who once referred to herself
ironically as a "magician of doubtful authenticity."

No doubt it must seem pedestrian to mention Joseph
Conrad in the presence of Anaïs Nin whose own name brings
to mind the symbolist poets, the surrealists, and Henry Miller, Djuna Barnes and Kenneth Patchen, and also James

Purdy. But Conrad knew the extent to which dreams are
suspect and also the extent to which they are true in Lord
Jim. Stein's comment on man--"He wants to be a saint,
and he wants to be a devil"--is a remark appropriate, I
think, to the visions of Anaïs Nin. And of course Conrad
also has his archetypal patterns, his dark Jungian construc-
tions, his myths, his ships that are whales, his Eden in
which Jim is a prisoner and Stein's own house which is the
underworld of the dead.

      Like Stephen who renounced "the lanterns of tradition"
in Stephen Hero, Anaïs Nin once wrote, referring to Joyce,
that "there is no need to seek a structure from the old myths.
In the unconscious itself, once unraveled, there is an indig-
enous structure and pattern. If we are able to detect and
seize and use it, we have the conflicts and forms of the novel
of the future." My own feeling is that anyone who knows that
we are as accurately as does Anaïs Nin is never very far
from the old myths. The title of her book-length prose poem,
The House of Incest, suggests her conscious preoccupation
with the double image, a preoccupation central to the core of
her work. The barque that sails to the sun and the barque
that sails to the moon; the drug of forgetfulness and the drug
of memory; the jail built within the church and the sister
kissing the shadow of her brother--these indicate something of
the nature of this constant imagination. "Like the failed photograph of the Mayan temple, in which by an accident, a failure to turn a small key, Lillian had been photographed both
standing up and lying down, and her head had seemed to lie
inside the jaws of a giant king snake of stone, and the stairs
of the pyramid to have been built across her body as if she
had been her own ghostly figure transcending the stone."

      Whatever the pain of the journey, the pain of immo-
bilization or of separation or of integration, and no matter
how refracting the mirrors or how warm or terrifying the
depths of the sea, there is a soft receptive actuality in the
prose of Anaïs Nin; to the extent that the reader becomes
the figure she has dreamed into existence, her work gives
back to us everything that is alive.

      However, if we wish to anticipate the voice of Anaïs
Nin, or to find an analogy for its sound, I think it better to
turn, not to the symbolists or surrealists or Conrad but,
rather, to "Twelfth Night." For a long while I have had the
irrational impression that when Viola first appears on the
beach she does so only after having been to the bottom of the

sea, that she did not leave the ship until it had sunk to the
bottom of the sea.   And I have the feeling that if Viola, this
ageless young woman who represents the highest form of love
and who is pretending to be her most loved brother, came to
us out of her dream, walking with her head turned back towards the disappearing garden and fading sea, and spoke to
the double image which is herself and ourselves also, the
voice we might overhear would be very much like the voice
of Anaïs Nin.

Albert J. Guerard (Harvard, 1961)

By all rights this afternoon should turn into a demonstration, a clamor, a public exhibition of outrage and delight;
it should become our moment of rebellious celebration when
at last we indulge our impulses for fist-shaking or revolver-
firing or cymbol-clashing, for cheering or for the tearing of
flesh....   Because, according to William Palmer, that youngest of anti-realists, Albert Guerard is "forsaking the ancient
east."   And surely now we should all be inspired to a final
afternoon of pleasure and revolt.   Perhaps there are Bacchae
among us, after all.   Only the Bacchae could prevent this departure from us and perhaps, before the end of the day, they
will.   I would like to think so.   Don't we deserve to perform,
in spirit at least, our rituals of homage, and shouldn't something, indicative of our pleasure and pain, happen to this
novelist, teacher, friend, father of three girls, between our
ancient and gloomy Sever Hall and the golden Pacific coast?

The worlds of Albert Guerard are the disparate ones
of Cambridge, Palo Alto, Paris--though we should not forget
the bar in Allston, the battlefield of an eastern European
country, the lonely and sinuous terrain of the south of France.
Ten years ago he was in Paris, having just returned from
Languedoc, that landscape of southern France which eventually
became a salty, symbolic marsh in The Bystander.   "I'm just
back this morning from four days in the south," he wrote in
May, 1951, "where I went to attend the annual convention of
the gypsies....   There were 7,000 of them plus 30,000 other
people ... in a town of less than a thousand ... and the discarded jerricans, tires, burnt-out charcoal fires and stinking
latrines would have done your heart good."   So here the man
who teaches the beauties and suasions of graceful prose, who
always encouraged every variety of younger writer, and who

has always taken care to stress "the notorious conservatism"
of his own fiction reveals all at once the true area of his
fictional sympathy. The packed humanity, the discarded tires
and gasoline tins and stinking latrines--these reflect his alle-
giance to the world of debilitation.

Of course there is truth as well as irony in "the notorious conservatism." Such a phrase might apply to the fiction of Mark Schorer and Glenway Wescott, who are among
the spiritual contemporaries of Albert Guerard; it might call
to mind the elaborate and sometimes sinister art of the psychological novelist; it might evoke the tensions and perfec-
tions of the novel as created by Conrad or Henry James.
There is psychic darkness enough in Conrad and James, and
no doubt it would be excessively irresponsible to force a comparison between the distortions of Albert Guerard and those
of, say, Nathanael West. And yet, when Nathanael West
drove from the east coast to California he said that the American deserts were filled with discarded tires; and all of us
know that Albert Guerard is not as notoriously conservative
a writer as he would have us believe.

His divided impulses emerge not only in the creation
of "world"--there is "psychic darkness" in the New England
community as well as in the squalid back streets of Nice--
but they emerge also in his treatment of the anti-hero as a
more or less conventional fictive character and as a grotesque. Along with the psychologically complex protagonist--
and this character is himself a figure tending toward absurdity
or neurosis, toward obsessive introspection, immobility, im-
potence--we find the peripheral character, the hapless grotesque, who is in fact the protagonist reduced to his essential helplessness or to the purity of his defenceless self. Albert Guerard has fashioned the grotesque into a pathetic and
comic bestial shade of the complex personality, fashioned him
into a Sancho Panza stripped of his good sense and grown in-
dolent, warmly flatulent. Felix Faber in Night Journey, the
soldier with the fat thighs and sagging buttocks, pink glisten-
ing head and flapping musette bag; or Clifton in The Bystander, ex-soldier and ex-black-marketeer with large hams and
bare brown head and sunken chest--these are the characters
at home in the world of "stinking latrines," and the characters on whom Albert Guerard most clearly spends his creative sympathies. In his latest novel, still in the final stages
of revision, the hapless grotesque--in this case Andrada, a
little political man wearing a great brown baggy suit--has all
but dispossessed the conventional complex protagonist.

However, while these novels enlarge the authenticity of the imaginative act, the contemporary flesh and blood anti-hero becomes the object of insufferable idealization. A recent New York Times Magazine photograph shows a young man with long dark hair and cow-like eyes, a snuffed cigarette caught between sensuous lips and the chain of a crucifix visible inside the collar of his striped shirt. He is a new French movie actor, and the caption reads: "Anti-Hero: Film star Jean-Paul Belmondo is no beauty. But his ugliness has the stamp of truth." Obviously we look to the Felix Fabers and Cliftons and Antonys and Andradas to save us from the humorless real life anti-hero of this disillusioned world.

By now some of the more unsettling resonances of this fiction writer have become myth; certainly by now the "pervasive influences" of this scholar and critic have become myth. And can the departure be tolerated after all? But we should remember the fiction writer's penchant for exaggeration and restraint and remember that it is not always necessary to destroy the hero in order to preserve him. From Cronin's to decorous Longfellow Hall, Harvard's unrecorded memory of its great teachers is indestructible. So after today it must be our pleasure, I think, to wait for trickling reports of the corruptibility of Stanford, reports of violence done to the west coast by the wisdom of the "ancient east," and reports too of the further novelistic achievements of Albert Guerard.

John Barth (Stanford, 1966)

John Barth comes from the Eastern Shore of Maryland, for some years was a member of the English Department of the University of Pennsylvania, and is now Professor of English at the State University of New York at Buffalo. His novels include The Floating Opera (1956), The End of the Road (1958), The Sot-Weed Factor (1960), and the recently published epic vision of contemporary life, Giles Goat-Boy.

A few conventional readers have been appalled by John Barth's sadistic humor; critics have praised his philosophical brilliance; journalists have attempted to cope with his shocking and gargantuan fictional achievement by labeling him

a Black Humorist. Quite rightly, John Barth has refused to
be identified with this "mythical" gang of Black Humorists--
serious writers do not flock together in popular schools.
But comic writer he obviously is, and I suspect that in the
distant future there already exists that unknown scholar
whose laborious research will one day reveal that John Barth
was actually born around the year 1550, was actually the un-
recognized contemporary of Cervantes and Rabelais, and,
though still living, yet still young, in the twentieth century,
was in fact the true inventor of the comic novel.

His purpose as a novelist is nothing less than to "reinvent the world" and to restore to contemporary literature
a proper Hero. With The Sot-Weed Factor and now Giles
Goat-Boy, John Barth has twice re-invented the world, has
twice given heroic shape to a novelistic voice which is unique
in this country and, at the same time, has about it a fantastic universal appeal. He pierces our most deplorable pre-
tensions--public and private--and, amazingly enough, in a
disintegrating world created for us a new literacy of the imagination.

The Sot-Weed Factor has been called:

a great delight of bawdiness and adventure,
begotten by Don Quixote upon Fanny Hill.

a moral allegory cloaked in terms of colonial history,
an epic farce,
a rowdy, ribald satire.

Giles Goat-Boy goes still further. But lest so much
bawdiness and pure creation sound too good to be true, we
should keep in mind what Mr. Barth said in a recent New
York Times interview: "My intention [in writing Giles Goat-
Boy] was to satirize the basic myth [of the Hero] and then,
hopefully, escalate the satire into something larger, darker,
and more compassionate." The most original and violent and
significant of comic visions, then, is the product of brooding
conscience.

A year ago, when John Barth read his fiction at the
YMHA Poetry Center in New York, a man in the audience
questioned the relevance of Mr. Barth's fiction to reality and
challenged his preoccupation with language. Mr. Barth re-
plied, simply, that "we writers would rather give up reality
than give up our language." And it is this language, the

sweep and rhythm and strength and involution of this particular voice, which accounts for much of the pleasure John
Barth's work gives to us and which defines him as a kind of
heroic, picaresque adventurer in innumerable landscapes of
pure prose.

It's a great pleasure to present Mr. John Barth.

Bernard Malamud (Brown, 1971)

        Once on a hot muggy night in Cambridge, Mass., I
found myself meeting Bernard Malamud's son and daughter,
who at the time were still young children. There was the
little girl, roundish, sweet, filled with radiant cheer; and
there was also the boy, slightly older, and dark-eyed, thin,
somber, aesthetic, who already played the cellow with severe
and lovely skill. The joy of meeting these two so very different children was immense--for themselves but also because, while shaking their hands I was thinking how like Bernard Malamud to do the impossible and to help to create his
children in the form of his fiction, since that great fiction
is also radiant and severe.

        In all that he has written, in The Magic Barrel, Idi-
ots First, Pictures of Fidelman, The Natural, The Assistant,
A New Life, The Fixer--commonplace experience becomes
mysterious, the possibilities of life and fiction both become
unlimited. Each fiction has its essential pain, its pure comedy, its flights into song.

        At the front of Pictures of Fidelman, that comic novel
about the painter, Arthur Fidelman, there are two epigraphs
which, together, are especially expressive of Bernard Malamud as man and artist; the first says:

        "The intellect of man is forced to choose
        Perfection of the life, or of the work..."

and is signed W. B. Yeats. The second says: "Both." and
is signed A. Fidelman. And of course behind the voice of
A. Fidelman we hear the great comic voice of B. Malamud.

        We're grateful to you, Bern, for being here.

INTRODUCTION

Concerning John Hawkes...

"Hawkes is one of the half dozen authors of first rank in America today."[1] So wrote Susan Sontag in 1964, the year for which Second Skin missed the National Book Award for fiction by only one vote.

Prior to this acclamation John Hawkes had written five short novels in addition to Second Skin, had distinguished himself by his participation in the Utah Writers' Conference (1962), the Aspen Institute for Humanistic Studies (1962), and the Bread Loaf Writers' Conference (1963), and had received a Guggenheim award, a National Institute of Arts and Letters grant (both in 1962), and a Ford Foundation grant (for 1964-5). In the eleven years that followed Hawkes wrote three more novels, four plays, several short stories, and various pieces of criticism. He rose to the rank of Professor of English and University Professor at Brown University, was writer-in-residence at the University of Virginia (April, 1965), a visiting lecturer at Stanford University (1966-7), and visiting professor at the City College of New York (1971-2), served on the Panel on Educational Innovation in Washington, D.C. (1966-7), and obtained a Rockefeller Fellowship (1966) and the French Prix du meilleur livre étranger for Les Oranges de Sang (The Blood Oranges; 1973).

Further accolades for Hawkes's work have also appeared in recent months. For example, Tony Tanner in his review of Travesty named Hawkes as "one of the very best living American writers."[2] Most significant, though, was the John Hawkes Symposium which took place at Muhlenberg College, Allentown, Pennsylvania on April 9-10, 1976. Here, an impressive group of scholars and critics, including Albert Guerard, Robert Scholes, Donald Greiner, John Graham, Frederick Busch, and Marcus Klein, strengthened by the presence of John Hawkes himself, discussed and criticized

9

nearly every aspect of the author's work through the reading of papers and panel and seminar discussions.

Yet, while Hawkes has enjoyed a long-lived and continuously growing reputation in academic circles and among literary critics here and abroad, he is neither widely-known to nor read by the reading public at large. Many would attribute this group's ignorance of and lack of appreciation, or outright distaste, for Hawkes's fiction and drama to the "difficulty" of these works. For, even in the early and middle fifties reviewers of Chairvari, The Cannibal, The Beetle Leg, and The Goose on the Grave emphasized the obscurity and incomprehensibility of these novels. Although later critics and reviewers more often praised Hawkes's style and imagination and stated that The Lime Twig and subsequent novels were more easily understood than the earlier works, many of them also admitted puzzlement over the meaning of the novels and warned readers of the need for slow contemplation and digestion of Hawkes's "darkly lyrical" passages.

Assuredly, the language of Hawkes's fiction everywhere weaves itself into magnificent metaphors, similes, and images in extremely precise phraseology, giving rise to widespread discussion of the poetic nature of the author's prose. Nonetheless, so nightmarish and macabre are Hawkes's fictive works that the phrase "Gothic novelist," applied to the author early in his career, would be accepted by many present-day critics as still an appropriate appellation.

"Surrealistic," "experimental," and "visionary" are other terms which have been used to describe Hawkes's fiction. All of these and similar designations have resulted, at least in part, from the novelist's disregard for conventional narrative structure. Thus, Hawkes utilizes no plot, shuffles past, present, and future events to acquire a feeling of timelessness, creates settings which smack of reality but are purely imaginary, and eschews normal character development. Indeed, as Hawkes himself explains it, the structure of his novels depends on "verbal and psychological coherence," based largely on "related or corresponding event, recurring images and recurring action."[3]

As can be imagined, then, Hawkes's style may well be mystifying to a considerable number of readers. On the other hand, Hawkes clarified his intentions in writing his novels, plays, and short stories in his interview with John Enck in 1965. "My aim," said the novelist, "has always been ...

never to let the reader (and myself) off the hook, so to
speak, never to let him think that the picture is any less
black than it is or that there is an easy way out of the nightmare of human existence."[4]   These intentions do not appear
to have changed perceptibly over the years.   Rather, they
have been buttressed from the beginning by Hawkes's feeling
of responsibility to "create and to throw into new light our
potential for violence and absurdity as well as for graceful
action."[5]

  Also, until a few years ago John Hawkes stressed the
comic elements of his novels in his interviews and readings.
In fact, Donald Greiner chose as the focal point of his mono-
graphic study of Hawkes's fiction the "comic terror" pervad-
ing these writings.[6]   But a recent article by Greiner on
Death, Sleep & the Traveler questions the existence of comedy in that work.   He sees, instead, Hawkes's successful com-
position of a "truly terrifying book" and alludes to a statement
from the author's "Notes on Writing a Novel"[7] to defend this
thesis.[8]

  However, if Greiner's new hypothesis is valid, what
are we to say about Travesty, Hawkes's youngest novel?
Does it lack "comic terror" and paint an even blacker, more
horrifying, picture of our existence?   Here, certainly, is
fertile ground for critics yet to be heard, some of whom, it
is hoped, will be aided by this bibliography.

  Surely, too, a careful reading of the four introductions
by Hawkes included in this volume will lend credence to argu-
ments for the novelist's stylistic artistry, or, at the very
least, will indicate that his powers of literary criticism are
considerable and should be borne in mind in the analysis of
any of his works.

Notes

1.   Susan Sontag, "A New Life for an Old One," New York
     Times Book Review, April 5, 1964, p. 5.

2.   Tony Tanner, Review of Travesty, New York Times
     Book Review, March 28, 1976, p. 24.

3.   John Enck, "John Hawkes: an Interview," Wisconsin
     Studies in Comparative Literature 6 (Summer 1965):
     11.

4. Ibid., p. 7.

5. Ibid., p. 6.

6. Donald J. Greiner, Comic Terror: the Novels of John
    Hawkes (Memphis: Memphis State University Press,
    1973).

7. See No. 63 in the bibliography for the full citation.

8. See No. 549 in the bibliography for the full citation to
    this article.

Concerning this bibliography...

    To aid researchers on the undergraduate level and be-
yond in any facet of the study of John Hawkes this bibliography was intended to be as comprehensive as possible. It is
composed mainly of published English-language materials
which contain statements about this novelist and his work and
which were discovered by myself prior to April, 1976. However, a considerable number of French-language items are
noted, along with several in other languages; a few non-print
materials, masters' theses and doctoral dissertations, two
unpublished bibliographies, and a collection of Hawkes's papers are included; and a number of early reviews of Travesty
and a few critical pieces, including the offerings which appeared in the April issue of Critique are inserted.

    Sources for the citations were many: 1) all known
published and unpublished bibliographies on Hawkes; 2) the
general and specialized indexes, bibliographies, dictionaries,
encyclopedias, and guides known by librarians to contain possible information on the career and work of modern American novelists, dramatists, and short story writers; 3) issues
of periodicals likely to publish articles or reviews on Hawkes
that were too recent to have been indexed; 4) the card catalog, accessions books, and unprocessed accessions file at
Harvard's Houghton Library; 5) a small file of newspaper reviews of Hawkes's plays located in the Harvard Theater Collection at the Nathan Marsh Pusey Library at Harvard, and
a similar, but slightly larger, file at the Theater Collection
of the Library and Museum of the Performing Arts of the
New York Public Library; 6) the card catalog at the John D.

Rockefeller, Jr. Library of Brown University; 7) correspondence with Caj Lundgren, Michael Pocalyko, representatives
of Harold Ober Associates, Inc. (Hawkes's agent), the Boston Globe, and the London Sunday Times; 8) certain articles
and books listed in the bibliography; and 9) the most important of all, John Hawkes himself, his personal library, and
especially his treasury of clippings of reviews and articles
from newspapers and other periodicals concerning his career
and writings. In fact, this latter collection of clippings was
the source of numerous unindexed reviews that would have
remained unknown to any interested researcher without ac-
cess to the collection, or now, to this bibliography. So too,
interlibrary loan proved to be a highly valuable means of ob-
taining copies of reviews and articles not found in Hawkes's
collection or in local libraries but cited in the published reference sources.

Unfortunately, the majority of the clippings located in
the novelist's collection and in the two theater files lacked
some vital pieces of bibliographic information which had to
be procured in various ways. In the search for these volume numbers, dates, authors' names, and page numbers several libraries were visited, including the Widener, Houghton,
and Pusey Libraries at Harvard, the John Hay and Rockefeller Libraries at Brown University, the Rhode Island Histori-
cal Society Library, Boston and Providence Public Libraries,
and, naturally, the Adams Library at Rhode Island College,
my present place of employment. Scores of letters were
written to individuals, newspaper, magazine, journal, and a
few book publishers, and libraries in the United States, Great
Britain, France, Switzerland, Sweden, and Denmark.

While the investigations often were quite fruitful, in-
tensive searching has not yet been successful in unearthing
complete information on approximately ten known items.
Three of these are included in the bibliography since only
one minor bit of information is missing in each and since a
personal search by a future researcher may bring to light
the information. These items are indicated by an asterisk
(*), placed immediately before the citation number.

As for the other six items, bibliographic information
is either so fragmentary or so uncertain that they have not
been given in this list. One of the elusive items is an article entitled, "Tapuzei Dam" (The Blood Oranges), by Rebec-
ca Rass, which appeared in the Friday supplement section
(page 23) of Tel-Aviv's Yedioth Ahronoth, perhaps in the

late summer or early fall of 1972.   Part interview with
Hawkes and part description and criticism of most of the author's novels through The Blood Oranges, this piece would
have been a valuable addition to the bibliography, had the
date been discovered.

All materials, with the exception of the Canadian editions of Hawkes's works, certain parts of the manuscript and
personal papers collection at Harvard, and the masters' theses and doctoral dissertations, were perused by myself.   The
purpose of such perusal was two-fold: to allow verification
of the bibliographic information and annotation of the materials.

Annotations, written in either the first or third person, have been provided for all items other than works edited by Hawkes, editions of Hawkes's novels, short fiction, and
plays, and theses and dissertations which demonstrate the extent of their concern with the author by their titles.   On the
other hand, notations of abstracts in Dissertation Abstracts
International have been appended to the dissertation citations.

Hopefully, the annotations offer fairly objective indica-
tions of the main ideas contained in the materials cited, as
well as the tone and general feeling of each of these pieces.
However, because most reviews can be assumed to present
plot summaries, such summaries are not generally noted in
the annotations of reviews.   Further, annotations of items in
French are entirely dependent upon my own translations,
while those of the Swedish and Danish items are based on
translations by native speakers of these two languages and the
Russian piece by a long-time student of Russian.

The basic arrangement of this bibliography organizes
citations under seven major headings, subdivided, in some
instances, into smaller divisions.   The progression is from
works by Hawkes to those partly by the novelist (interviews)
to those, finally, about him.   Under PART I, Works by
Hawkes, the items of subdivisions A through E and G are
listed chronologically.   All other parts use alphabetical arrangement.   The only exception to this procedure occurs in
PART I. A, where all English-language editions of a particular novel by Hawkes are grouped together in chronological order before editions in other languages are listed.

Generally, the bibliographic style suggested by Kate
L. Turabian in her fourth edition of A Manual for Writers of

Term Papers, Theses, and Dissertations (Chicago: University of Chicago Press, 1973) has been followed. Where deviations from this style have been made, they have been adopted with the intention of being as helpful as possible to the reader. For example, the inverted dates for newspaper and magazine citations (e.g., 4 April 1976) have not been used. In another case, city names have not been placed in front of certain newspaper titles, as would be necessary according to Turabian, because the result would have been forms of titles that would be needlessly confusing. Examples of such titles are the Radcliffe News, Harvard Crimson, and the Brown Daily Herald, all easily recognized without the addition of city names.

Followed closely, though, are Turabian's rulings on the types of information to be included for newspapers, weekly magazines, and magazines of general interest. "Magazines of general interest" are here understood to be those periodicals, excluding newspapers, which are well-known and widely read by the general adult reading public in the country in which these periodicals are published. William Katz's second edition of Magazines for Libraries (New York: R. R. Bowker, 1972) was consulted on occasion for aid in determining whether or not certain periodicals fit this definition. When Katz and a few other pertinent reference sources failed to help, the bibliographic information requisite for a journal article was employed in the citation in question.

Most entries have been made under the names of authors or editors. Where the names of a few authors have been supplied as a result of personal contacts or correspondence and do not appear anywhere in the cited material, these names are enclosed in brackets.

The form of an author's or editor's name given in an entry in most cases is that which actually appears in the item. In several instances, however, when more than one item by the same author has been included in the bibliography, the fullest form of the author's name found in any of the pieces is used in the citations for all of the items. So, too, where correspondence has brought to light an author's full name in a case in which only initials were previously known, the full name has been used in the citation, and parentheses have been placed around those elements of the name not actually revealed by the item.

A number of citations are also followed by numbers

enclosed in brackets. These are the numbers of the pages
on which one or more works by Hawkes are treated specifically when the page numbers in the citation proper are those
for a review or article devoted to one or more works other
than Hawkes's.

"See also" references, located at the end of various
subdivisions of this bibliography, point out material that
might otherwise be overlooked on a particular topic and, it
is hoped, add to the usefulness of this work. The name and
periodical indexes, placed at the end of this volume, should
also enhance the accessibility of the list.

A few additional remarks concerning the individual
parts of the bibliography are necessary at this point:

In Part I, Works by Hawkes, the author of each item
is assumed to be John Hawkes except where it is obvious
that Hawkes is not the understood entry element. The brack-
eted dates which appear in Numbers 2 and 51 are the true
dates of publication and have been determined from information culled from correspondence with the publisher and notices of publication found in the New York Times and New
York Herald Tribune.

Part II, Interviews with Hawkes, includes articles
that are direct interviews with the novelist, as well as those
comprised of statements resulting from interviews. Number
75 is an example of the latter instance.

Part III lists materials offering information about the
life and/or career of the author. A possible Hawkes biogra-
pher may even be helped by the inclusion of notices of the
honors accorded to Hawkes at various times.

Part IV, Reviews of Hawkes's works, has within its
bounds all newspaper and other articles written with the intention of giving readers unfamiliar with the reviewed works
the opinions of other readers, sometimes literary critics,
about these writings. Anonymous reviews are entered under
the phrase: Review of (name of work). Similarly, when a
review of a work appears as a separately treated item in a
review column, the phrase, Review of (name of work), is inserted where the title of a review normally would be placed.

The symbols attached to the citations are a particularly important feature of this part of the bibliography.

These symbols indicate the approximate lengths of the reviews or parts of review articles concerned with Hawkes's work.   The key to the symbols is as follows:

no symbol	- less than 150 words
o	- 150 to 300 words
-	- 300 to 500 words
+	- 500 to 1000 words
*	- 1000 to 2000 words
#	- 2000 words and over.

Part V was created to encompass all published items, other than reviews, that present critical statements about Hawkes's work.   Subsection D, Lectures/Readings, lists articles that report the contents of certain lectures and readings by the author.   Not only do they contain remarks by the authors of the pieces but also many quotations from Hawkes's own comments about his writing.   Subsection A's "see also" references similarly include references to items (other than reviews) in which the novelist speaks about one or more of his works.   These items are distinguished from the others by being underlined.

The last section, Part VII, Hawkes Bibliographies, cites those bibliographies which were consulted during the preparation of this listing, excluding those which have merely a handful of items.   The reader ought to be alerted also to the fact that as this bibliography goes to the publisher, two other published bibliographies on Hawkes should be appearing.   One is a fairly lengthy annotated bibliography by Robert M. Scotto of Baruch College of the City University of New York.   Mr. Scotto's Hawkes bibliography will be published by Garland Publishing Company in the same volume as bibliographies on Heller and Pynchon.   The other bibliography is my own checklist of reviews of The Blood Oranges, Death, Sleep & the Traveler, and Travesty compiled from the bibliography in hand.   This checklist, entitled "The Seventies Triad: a Checklist of Reviews," will accompany papers presented at the Muhlenberg Symposium on John Hawkes in a volume to be published by New Directions Press.

Acknowledgments

It would be virtually impossible for me to name all of the fine people who helped in a variety of ways with this bibliography. Yet, some should be mentioned to whom I owe very special thanks.

Above all, there are John and Sophie Hawkes, whose unfailing aid and encouragement have gently nudged me through several years of sporadic compilation.

Then, there are the representatives of New Directions Press, Chatto & Windus, Stig Vendelkaers Forlag, Harold Ober Associates, and the Literary Guild of America; George MacBeth, former Producer of Talks and Documentaries for the British Broadcasting Corporation; Eric Kirkland of the Radio-Television Center, School of Continuing Education, University of Virginia; Marshall C. Olds, a graduate student in 1975 at Case Western Reserve University; Michael Pocalyko, a student at Muhlenberg College in 1976, and Caj Lundgren of Svenska Dagbladet, all of whom either responded readily to my letters with extremely informative replies and/or materials or sent letters and materials voluntarily.

Quite indispensable was the aid cheerfully given by Hadassah and Jerome Stein, Doris Karlsson, Jenny Van Pelt, Maria Chart, and Sandra Gallup. Their translations enabled me to provide confident comments and annotations about several foreign materials on Hawkes.

It is a pleasure, too, to render thanks to certain colleagues, former mentors, and brothers and sisters in the library world. Two of my colleagues, Richard A. Olsen, Director of the James P. Adams Library at Rhode Island College, and Lucille Sibulkin, Head of Technical Services at the same library, eased the rigors of my research with their kind interest and tangible assistance; Walter T. Dziura and Juan R. Freudenthal, both of the Simmons College School of Library Science, gave me wise instruction in the compilation of bibliographies that is, I hope, witnessed in the present work; and the staffs of the Adams Library of Rhode Island College, the Rockefeller and Hay Libraries of Brown University, the Widener, Houghton, and Pusey Libraries of Harvard University, the Bibliothèque Nationale, the Library of Congress, the British Library, and the Theater Collection of the Library and Museum of the Performing Arts at the New York Public Library all bestowed upon me library services of superior quality.

In addition, I am greatly indebted to the scores of librarians and library assistants, representatives of newspapers and periodicals, and other individuals who expended their time and effort to answer my letters seeking bits and pieces of information.

Finally, there are the friends and relatives who have helped to make the rocky road to publication a little smoother. A word of glad thanks to them all and especially to my patient and thoughtful grandmother.

C. A. H.

THE BIBLIOGRAPHY

PART I

WORKS BY HAWKES

A. NOVELS

1. "Charivari." New Directions in Prose and Poetry 11
   (1949): 365-436; reprinted in Lunar Landscapes
   (No. 34).

2. The Cannibal. Introduction by Albert J. Guerard.
   Direction 13. Norfolk, Conn. : New Directions,
   [1950] c1949; 1st rev. Amer. ed., New York:
   New Directions, 1962; paperback ed. , New York:
   New Directions, 1962.

2a. _____. London: Neville Spearman, 1962; reissue,
    London: Chatto & Windus, 1968; paperback ed. ,
    London: Sphere Books, 1970.

2b. Människoataren. Översattning av Berit ock Ingvar
    Skogsberg. Stockholm: Tidens Forlag, 1962.
    [Swedish]

2c. Kannibalen. Oversat af Henrik Bering Liisberg.
    Fredensborg: Arena, 1965. [Danish, paperback]

2d. Le Cannibale; Roman. Traduit de l'Américain par
    René Daillie. Les Lettres nouvelles. Paris:
    Denoël, 1972. [French, paperback]
    SELECTIONS: Nos. 10, 19, 25.

3. The Beetle Leg. New York: New Directions, 1951;
   paperback ed. , New York: New Directions, 1967.

3a. _____. London: Chatto & Windus, 1967.
    SELECTION: No. 26.

4. The Goose on the Grave [and The Owl]; Two Short
   Novels. New York: New Directions, 1954; re-

23

printed in Lunar Landscapes (No. 34).
SELECTIONS: Nos. 12, 13, 14.

5.   The Lime Twig. With an introduction by Leslie A.
     Fiedler. New York: New Directions, 1961; pa-
     perback ed., New York: New Directions, 1961;
     limited edition (100 copies), New York: New Di-
     rections, 1963.

5a. _____. Don Mills, Ontario: Burns & MacEachern,
     1962.

5b. _____. London: Neville Spearman, 1962; reissue,
     London: Chatto and Windus, 1968; paperback ed.,
     London: Sphere Books, 1970.

5c. Le Gluau; Roman. Traduit de l'Américain par Aanda
     Golem. Les Lettres nouvelles, 34. Paris: René
     Julliard, 1963. [French, paperback]

5d. Die Leimrute. Deutsch von Grete Weil. Limes nova,
     6. Wiesbaden: Limes Verlag, 1964. [German,
     paperback]
     SELECTIONS: Nos. 15, 16, 33, 36.

6.   Second Skin. New York: New Directions, 1964; pa-
     perback ed., New York: New Directions, 1964;
     limited edition (100 copies), New York: New Di-
     rections, 1964; paperback ed., New York: New
     American Library, 1965.

6a. _____. Toronto: McClelland & Stewart, 1964.
     [paperback]

6b. _____. London: Chatto and Windus, 1966; paper-
     back ed., London: Chatto and Windus, 1966; pa-
     perback ed., London: Sphere Books, 1968.

6c. Seconda Pelle, Romanzo. [Traduzione dall'Inglese di
     Attilio Veraldi.] Milan: Feltrinelli, 1967. [Ital-
     ian]

6d. Cassandra; Roman. Traduit de l'Américain par Jac-
     queline Bernard. [Preface par Peter Brooks.]
     Les Lettres nouvelles. Paris: Denoël, 1968.
     [French, paperback]

6e.   Toinen Nahka. Suomentanut Matti Rossi. Helsinki:
        Werber Söderström Osakeyhtiö-Porvoo, 1968.
        [Finnish, paperback]

6f.   Die zweite Haut; Roman. [Aus dem Amerikanischen
        von Walter Hasenclever.] Cologne, Berlin: Kie-
        penheuer & Witsch, 1971. [German]

6g.   Segunda Piel. Versión española de Amalia Castro y
        Alberto Manguel. Narradores de Hoy, 39. Buenos
        Aires: Centro Editor de America Latina, 1972.
        [Spanish, paperback]
        SELECTIONS: Nos. 23, 27, 29, 31, 32.

7.   The Blood Oranges. New York: New Directions, 1971;
        paperback ed., New York: New Directions, 1972.

7a.   _____. Toronto: McClelland & Stewart, 1971; pa-
        perback ed., Toronto: McClelland & Stewart,
        1972.

7b.   _____. London: Chatto & Windus, 1971.

7c.   Les Oranges de Sang; Roman. Traduit de l'Américain
        par Alain Delahaye. Les Lettres nouvelles.
        Paris: Denoël, 1973. [French, paperback]
        Received Le Prix du Meilleur Livre Etranger in
        1973.

7d.   Arazzo d'Amore. Traduzione di Camillo Pennati.
        Torino: Einaudi, 1974. [Italian]

7e.   Las Naranjas sangrientas. [Traducción: Amalia Cas-
        tro y Alberto Manguel.] Buenos Aires: Ediciones
        del Sol, 1975. [Spanish, paperback]
        SELECTIONS: Nos. 35, 38, 39, 40, 41, 42.

8.   Death, Sleep and the Traveler. New York: New Di-
        rections, 1974; paperback ed., New York: New
        Directions, 1975.

8a.   _____. Toronto: McClelland & Stewart, 1974; pa-
        perback ed., Toronto: McClelland & Stewart,
        1975.

8b.   _____. London: Chatto & Windus, 1975.

8c.   La Morte, le Sommeil et un Voyageur; Roman. Tra-
       duit de l'Américain par Jacqueline Bernard. Les
       Lettres nouvelles. Paris: Denoël, 1975.
       [French, paperback]

8d.   A Morte, o Sono e o Viajante. Tradução: Reinaldo
       Bairão e José Carlos Campanha. Série Ficção
       Imago. Rio de Janeiro: Imago Editora, 1975.
       [Portuguese, paperback]
       SELECTIONS: Nos. 44, 45, 46.

9.   Travesty. New York: New Directions, 1976.

9a.   _____. Toronto: McClelland & Stewart, 1976.

9b.   _____. London: Chatto & Windus, 1976.

9c.   Mimodrame; Roman. Traduit de l'Américain par Mi-
       chel Jaworski. Les Lettres nouvelles. Paris:
       Denoël, 1976. [French, paperback]
       SELECTIONS: Nos. 47, 48.

B.   SHORT FICTION

10.   "Death of a Maiden." Wake, No. 6 (Spring 1948),
       pp. 85-96. (From The Cannibal)

11.   "Death of an Airman." New Directions in Prose and
       Poetry 12 (1950): 261-6; reprinted in Lunar
       Landscapes (No. 34).

12.   "The Courtier." New Directions in Prose and Poetry
       13 (1951): 236-45. (From The Goose on the
       Grave)

13.   "The Lay Brothers." New Directions in Prose and
       Poetry 14 (1953): 281-7. (From The Goose on
       the Grave)

14.   "Die Laienbrüder." In Junge Amerikanische Literatur,
       pp. 168-76. Hrsg. Walter Hasenclever. Ullstein
       Buch, Nr. 241. West Berlin: Ullstein Bücher,
       1959. (From The Goose on the Grave)

15.   "The Horse in a London Flat." Accent 20 (Winter

1960): 3-19; reprinted in Accent; an Anthology, 1940-60, pp. 93-109. Edited by Daniel Curley, George Scouffas, Charles Shattuck. Urbana: University of Illinois Press, 1973. (From The Lime Twig)

16. "The Lodging House Fires." Audience 7 (Spring 1960): 61-77. (From The Lime Twig)

17. "The Grandmother." New Directions in Prose and Poetry 17 (1961): 51-64; reprinted in Lunar Landscapes (No. 34).

18. "The Traveler." MSS 1 (Winter 1962): 166-75; reprinted in New Directions in Prose and Poetry 18 (1964): 162-70; and in Lunar Landscapes (No. 34).

19. "Las Cruces." Papeles de son Armadans 74 (May 1962): 169-86. (From The Cannibal. Version de Jorge A. Franco Irizarri, corregida por Jorge C. Trulock y Anthony Kerrigan)

20. "A Song Outside." San Francisco Review, No. 1 (June 1962), pp. 4-9; reprinted in Lunar Landscapes (No. 34).

21. "A Little Bit of the Old Slap and Tickle." Noble Savage, No. 5 (October 1962), pp. 19-23; reprinted in Harvard Advocate 104 (October 2, 1970): 7-8; and in Lunar Landscapes (No. 34).

22. "Two Shoes for One Foot." Emerson Review 1 (Winter 1963): 26-34.

23. "Honeymoon Hideaway (circa 1944)." Texas Quarterly 6 (Summer 1963): 20-32. (From Second Skin)

24. "The Nearest Cemetery." San Francisco Review Annual, No. 1, o.s. No. 14 (Fall 1963), pp. 178-85; reprinted in Write and Rewrite; a Study of the Creative Process, pp. 266-72 (See No. 29); in Creative Writing and Rewriting, pp. 266-72 (See No. 29); in Lunar Landscapes (No. 34); and in The Merrill Studies in Second Skin, pp. 38-43 (No. 537).

25. "Riot at the Institution." In A New Directions Read-
     er, pp. 136-42. Edited by Hayden Carruth and
     J. Laughlin. Norfolk, Conn.: New Directions,
     1964 (pa.); Toronto: McClelland & Stewart, 1964.
     (From The Cannibal)

26. "Sarcophagus of Mud." In The Personal Voice; a
     Contemporary Prose Reader, pp. 587-91. Edited
     by A. J. Guerard et al. Philadelphia: J. P.
     Lippincott Co., 1964. (From The Beetle Leg)

27. "The Heart Demands Satisfaction." Vogue, January
     15, 1964, pp. 72-3, 75, 112.

28. "En mundsmag fra de hjemlige kødgryder." In Ny
     amerikansk prosa, pp. 86-90. Redigeret af Erik
     Wiedemann. Copenhagen: Stig Vendelkaers for-
     lag, 1966. (Tr. into Danish by Maria Marcus of
     "A Little Bit of the Old Slap and Tickle")

29. "Drag Race on the Beach." In Write and Rewrite: a
     Study of the Creative Process, pp. 277-83. Edit-
     ed by John Kuehl. New York: Meredith Press,
     1967; In Creative Writing and Rewriting, pp. 277-
     83. Edited by John Kuehl. New York: Apple-
     ton-Century-Crofts, 1967. (From Second Skin)

30. "From: The Cannibal." In The World of Black Hu-
     mor; an Introductory Anthology of Selections and
     Criticism, pp. 66-81. Edited by Douglas M.
     Davis. New York: E. P. Dutton, 1967.

31. "The Gentle Island." In Write and Rewrite: a Study
     of the Creative Process, pp. 273-76 (See No. 29);
     In Creative Writing and Rewriting, pp. 273-76
     (See No. 29). (From Second Skin)

32. "Peau neuve." Les Lettres nouvelles (October-No-
     vember 1967): 25-35. (From Second Skin.
     Translated into French by Jacqueline Bernard)

33. "Hencher." In The Single Voice, pp. 176-93. Edited
     by Jerome Charyn. New York: Macmillan (Col-
     lier Books), 1969; paperback ed., London: Col-
     lier-Macmillan, 1969. (From The Lime Twig)

34. Lunar Landscapes; Stories & Short Novels, 1949-1963.

New York: New Directions, 1969; limited edition
(150 copies), New York: New Directions, 1969.
paperback ed., New York: New Directions, 1969.

34a.   _____. Toronto: McClelland & Stewart, 1969.

34b.   _____. London: Chatto and Windus, 1970.
        Contains the stories and short novels listed under
        Nos. 1, 4, 11, 17, 18, 20, 21, and 24.

35.   "Burnt Orange." Dutton Review, No. 1 (1970), pp.
        137-50. (From The Blood Oranges)

36.   "John Hawkes: Le Gluau [a Brief Extract]." Informa-
        tions & Documents, No. 291 (March 1-15, 1970),
        p. 45. (From the French translation of The Lime
        Twig)

37.   "Permis med Frugan." Svenska Dagbladet (Stockholm),
        April 26, 1970, p. 18. (Translation by Caj Lund-
        gren into Swedish of "A Little Bit of the Old Slap
        and Tickle")

38.   "From a Forthcoming Novel." Harvard Advocate 104
        (October 2, 1970): 5. (From The Blood Oranges)

39.   "From The Blood Oranges." Works in Progress, No.
        2 (1971), pp. 221-37.

40.   "From The Blood Oranges." TriQuarterly, No. 20
        (Winter 1971), pp. 113-29. (From The Blood Or-
        anges)

41.   "Kissing the Goat-girl." Antaeus, No. 3 (Autumn
        1971), pp. 7-23. (From The Blood Oranges)

42.   "Swapping." Fiction 1 (Spring 1972): 19-20. (From
        The Blood Oranges)

43.   "The Universal Fears." AR; American Review, No.
        16 (February 1973), pp. 108-23; reprinted in Su-
        per-fiction, or the Story Transformed, pp. 113-
        28. Edited by Joe David Bellamy. New York:
        Vintage Books, 1975.

44.   "The Ship." Fiction 1, No. 4 ([May] 1973): 22-5.
        (From Death, Sleep and the Traveler)

45.   "The Animal Eros." Antaeus, No. 13/14 (Spring/
       Summer 1974), pp. 70-8. (From Death, Sleep
       and the Traveler)

46.   "In Dante's Forest." AR; American Review, No. 20
       (April 1974), pp. 60-70. (Adapted from Death,
       Sleep and the Traveler)

47.   "Dead Passion." Fiction 4, No. 1 ([Fall?] 1975):
       17-9. (From Travesty)

48.   "Design and Debris." TriQuarterly, No. 35, [Part]
       1: Minute Stories (Winter 1976), pp. 7-9. (From
       Travesty)

C. PLAYS

49.   "The Wax Museum." In Plays for a New Theater;
       Playbook 2, pp. 101-20. New York: New Direc-
       tions, 1966; reprinted in The Innocent Party (No.
       51).

       PRODUCTIONS:
           a.   Theater Company of Boston, April 28-May 1,
       May 3-7, 1966. Directed by David Wheeler. Pre-
       sented at the Hotel Touraine in its Festival of New
       American Plays.
           b.   Chelsea Theater (Brooklyn Academy of Music),
       April 4-5, 11-12, 1969. Directed by Larry Loonin.
           c.   "Das Wachsfigurenkabinett." Theater an der
       Grenze (Kreuzlingen, Switzerland), May, 1969. Trans-
       lated by Marianne Driessen and staged by Frederick
       Ribell.
           d.   The Assembly Theater (New York City), No-
       vember 28-29, December 1, 5, 6, 8, 1969. Directed
       by Terry Walker.
           e.   The Roundabout Theatre (New York City), July,
       1972. A showcase production by Dan Levine.
           f.   Athens New Theatre (Athens, Greece), May,
       1974.

50.   "The Undertaker." Harvard Advocate 100 (Fall 1966):
       4-14; reprinted in The Innocent Party (No. 51)

PRODUCTIONS:
    a. Theater Company of Boston, March 28, 1967.
Directed by David Wheeler.
    b. The Assembly Theater (New York City), November 28-29, December 1, 5, 6, 8, 1969. Directed by Terry Walker.

51.   The Innocent Party: Four Short Plays. Preface by
        Herbert Blau. New York: New Directions,
        [1967] c1966; paperback ed., New York: New Directions, [1967] c1966.

51a.   _____. Toronto: McClelland & Stewart, [1967]
        c1966.

51b.   _____. London: Chatto and Windus, 1967.
        Includes The Innocent Party, The Questions, The
        Undertaker, and The Wax Museum.

PRODUCTIONS of The Innocent Party:
    a. Theater Company of Boston, February, 1968.
Directed by David Wheeler.
    b. Chelsea Theater (Brooklyn Academy of Music),
April 4-5, 11-12, 1969. Directed by Larry Loonin.
    c. Gramercy Arts Theater, November 30-December 5, 1971. Directed by William E. Hunt. A privately-produced presentation for which no admission fee was charged.

PRODUCTIONS of The Questions:
    a. Stanford Repertory Theater, January 13-16,
1966. Directed by Robert Laber.
    b. NBC Television, April, 1967. An hour show
on the drama series, "Experiment."
    c. Trinity Repertory Theater, Providence, R.I.,
February 17-25, 1967. Directed by Adrian Hall.

D. POETRY

52.   Fiasco Hall. Cambridge, Mass.: Harvard University
        Printing Office, 1943. [Privately printed]
        Contents: "To My Mother and Father," "Elderbury Lane," "Journey," "In Malice Bred," "The Plea," "Sweet Tomb in Mist," "Zu meinem Schatz," "The Beggar," "His Life," "Mid Winter's Walk," "Rising

Moon," "Last Chant," "Aus meiner Herzfreude."
   These thirteen poems were written by Hawkes during his years in high school and were printed while
he was at Harvard. Approximately forty of the one
hundred copies printed still exist. Two copies are
located in the John Hay Library at Brown University
and one at Harvard's Houghton Library.

53.   "Little Beatrice." Harvard Advocate 130 (April 28,
         1947): 12; reprinted in Harvard Advocate Centen-
         nial Anthology, pp. 270-1. Edited by Jonathan
         D. Culler. Cambridge, Mass.: Schenkman Pub-
         lishing Co., 1966.

54.   "The Magic House of Christopher Smart." Harvard
         Advocate 130 (May 21, 1947): 14.

E.   CRITICAL PIECES

55.   "Notes on Violence." Audience 7 (Spring 1960): 60.
         Thought-provoking comments in praise of the ex-
perimental novel because of its unsympathetic stance
and humor arising "from half-recollected injuries or
desires."

56.   "The Voice of Edwin Honig." Voices; a Journal of
         Poetry, No. 174 (January-April 1961), pp. 39-47.
         Intense, artfully-constructed criticism of Honig's
poetry. Deems this poetry to be "moral and satiric,"
filled with language "thick with death," conjuring up
"frequent visions of houses," and promoting nightmare
imagery.

57.   "Flannery O'Connor's Devil." Sewanee Review 70
         (Summer 1962): 395-407; reprinted in Flannery
         O'Connor, pp. 25-37. Edited by Robert E. Reiter.
         St. Louis: B. Herder Book Co., 1968.
         For the most part compares the use of satire by
Nathanael West and Flannery O'Connor. Finds that
these two writers both depict man as an irrational
creature and choose the devil as a major theme. De-
termines, moreover, that O'Connor's view coincides
with her devil's view and that her use of image and
symbol is "mildly perverse."

58.   "Notes on The Wild Goose Chase." Massachusetts
        Review 3 (Summer 1962): 784-8; reprinted in
        The American Novel since World War II, pp. 247-
        51. Edited by Marcus Klein. Greenwich, Conn. :
        Fawcett Publications, 1969; and in The Merrill
        Studies in Second Skin, pp. 20-3 (No. 537).
        Much-quoted and analyzed comments on fiction
    and on the purpose of the novel.

59.   "William Palmer; a Genesis West Presentation (8)."
        Genesis West 3 (Winter 1965): 16-7.
        An introduction to selections from Palmer's Coy-
    haique.

60.   "The Critics, Writers & Editors..." Washington
        Post, September 26, 1965, Book Week, pp. 6-7,
        18, 20, 22, 24-5. [7, 25] Hawkes gives a short reply of about one hundred
        words to a survey taken concerning the best authors
        of the 1945-65 period. He reveals his view that the
        postwar American novel has "developed mainly in
        terms of verbal and visionary liberation."
            Paul West's statement on page 25, defending his
        nomination of Hawkes for inclusion in this list of best
        authors, praises Hawkes's "articulate, complicated vi-
        sion which is rarely overwritten or wilfully involved."

61.   "Story into Novel: [Introduction and] Commentary."
        In Write and Rewrite: a Story of the Creative
        Process, pp. 265, 284-7. Edited by John Kuehl.
        New York: Meredith Press, 1967; in Creative
        Writing and Rewriting, pp. 265, 284-7. Edited
        by John Kuehl. New York: Appleton-Century-
        Crofts, 1967; reprinted with slight abbreviation in
        The Merrill Studies in Second Skin, pp. 35-8 (No.
        537).
            A discussion of the development of Second Skin in
        which "The Nearest Cemetery" (No. 24) is shown to
        be a preliminary "vision" of this novel.

61a.   An Experiment in Teaching Writing to College Fresh-
        men (Voice Project). [Washington, D.C.]: U.S.
        Department of Health, Education, and Welfare,
        Office of Education, Bureau of Research, 1967;
        microfiche and hard copy reprints, Bethesda,
        Maryland: ERIC Document Reproduction Service,
        EDO18 442 [1968].

This is the final report of the Voice Project, directed by Hawkes at Stanford University during the 1966-7 academic year and sponsored by the U.S. Department of Health, Education, and Welfare (Project No. 6-2075-24, Contract No. OEC-4-6-062075-1180). Submitted in October, 1967, it also appears to have been printed without the initial summary section in August, 1967 under the title: Voice Project: an Experiment in Teaching Writing to College Freshmen (No. 61b).

The report includes a summary of the Project (pp. x-xviii); an introductory section by the novelist ("The Voice Project at Stanford," pp. xix-xlvii), discussing the background, objectives, methods, and findings of the Project; four papers written in August, 1965 at the Tufts Seminar to Initiate New Experiments in Undergraduate Instruction, one being Hawkes's original proposal for the Voice Project ("The Voice Project," pp. 18-22); a reconstruction of the classes of one of the sections ("The Classroom Experience: John Hawkes and Zeese Papanikolas. Log by Zeese Papanikolas," p. 24-130), along with logs of a few sessions of other sections at the university, high school, and junior high levels; a description of the pre-college summer section; a selection of assignments and student writings; and appendices containing lists of consultants and participants and reports on the Project at Stanford and in the local schools.

Number 62 provides a briefer description of the Voice Project, derived from this report.

61b.   Voice Project: an Experiment in Teaching Writing to College Freshmen. John Hawkes, Project Director [et al]. Palo Alto?: Stanford University?, 1967.

        See 61a for remarks on this report.

62.   "The Voice Project: an Idea for Innovation in the Teaching of Writing." In Writers as Teachers; Teachers as Writers, pp. 89-144. Edited and with an introd. by Jonathan Baumbach. New York: Holt, Rinehart and Winston, 1970.

        In the first section (pp. 89-103) Hawkes describes the origin and aims of the Voice Project, hosted by Stanford University during the 1966-67 academic year and funded by DHEW, along with his conclusions and recommendations. Essentially, the Project aimed at

encouraging "the non-fiction writing student to discover himself as the center of a writing process which results in a personal or identifiable prose, rather than in 'machine' or 'voiceless' prose."
Pages 103-10, "The Classroom Experience: Some Examples," by John Hawkes and Zeese Papanikolas, presents an account of two typical class meetings during the Project as recalled and reflected upon by Z. Papanikolas, who kept a log of the sessions. The account includes Hawkes's comments on student work and a passage written by Hawkes for class use.
See No. 61a for the full report of the Project, from which this account was drawn.

63.   "Notes on Writing a Novel." Brown Alumni Monthly 73 (January 1973): 9-16; a slightly different version in TriQuarterly, No. 30 (Spring 1974), pp. 109-26.
In explaining his purpose in writing novels Hawkes includes several pieces of biographical information on himself and provides an account of the genesis of Second Skin. He emphasizes the source of the two islands in the novel and the relationship of the story, "The Nearest Cemetery" (No. 24), to the novel.

64.   Bourjaily, Vance. "That Stories Should Not Be Their Own Reward." New York Times Book Review, August 5, 1973, p. 27.
In talking about encouraging short fiction writing and, specifically, about the Iowa Short Fiction Prize for 1973, Bourjaily quotes a few sentences from Hawkes's remarks given in judgment of H. E. Francis's Itinerary of Beggars, the winner of the 1973 Iowa Prize. Hawkes praises Francis's splendid treatment of the theme of "the oneness of all things."

65.   "Barth, L'Opera flottant et moi." Informations & Documents, No. 341 (May 1974), pp. 35-8. (Translated by Alain Delahaye)
Hawkes admires Barth's ability to choose the proper word ("le mot juste") and his remarkable manipulations of voice. He compares Barth and Nabokov with respect to their use of mental derangement to arrive at aesthetic felicity ("bonheur esthetique") in their writing. He further notes that in The Floating Opera (analyzed here at some length) Barth, evidently, wishes to clothe the abstractions of the human voice with the

comic habits of humanity--to reinvent the language of
the world.

66.   "The Floating Opera and Second Skin." Mosaic 8
      (Fall 1974): 17-28.
      In this version of a lecture given at Stanford in
      1966 Hawkes begins by comparing Barth to himself.
      While pointing out the differences and similarities be-
      tween The Floating Opera and Second Skin, he com-
      ments that both Barth and himself "work with materi-
      als of psychic or cerebral derangement in our efforts
      to arrive at aesthetic bliss." He devotes a lengthy
      discussion to the centralized working requirement in
      both novels: "the shadow of the self-inflicted death of
      the father."

SEE ALSO: Nos. 540, 546.

F.   SPECIAL LIBRARY COLLECTION OF UNPUBLISHED
     MATERIALS

67.   Cambridge, Massachusetts. Harvard University.
      Houghton Library. [Manuscripts and papers of
      John Hawkes].
      As of May, 1976 the Houghton Library houses
      numerous typescripts, galley proofs, and page proofs
      of Hawkes's works, which were deposited by New Di-
      rections and which, with few exceptions, are re-
      stricted. Houghton's accessions record *68M-107
      (found in Houghton Library Accessions 1968-1969,
      vol. 3, 68M-1 - 68M-180) also indicates a deposit of
      papers by Hawkes in April, 1969. These papers are
      not restricted and include, most importantly, a multi-
      tude of letters to and from Hawkes (among them,
      thirty-four from Albert Guerard, thirty from Flan-
      nery O'Connor, and two hundred ninety-seven from
      James Laughlin) and manuscripts of some of Hawkes's
      published and unpublished works (stories, poems, a
      play entitled Malady from 1947, and critical pieces).
      Houghton accession record *73M-67 reports the
      deposit by Hawkes in June, 1973 of "Thirty-seven
      Letters to John C. B. Hawkes; 1944-1945," although
      the entry cites the inclusion in this deposit of other
      letters, a typescript of an unpublished work, Lilli
      Marlene, and two other manuscripts not by Hawkes.

These materials can only be seen with the novelist's permission.

Later on in 1973 (November), Mrs. Gordon Cairnie deposited three letters written by Hawkes to her husband, Gordon Cairnie of the Grolier Book Shop, in 1961 and 1962. These letters, cited in accession record #73M-69, are unrestricted.

G. MISCELLANEOUS

68. The Personal Voice; a Contemporary Prose Reader. Edited by A. J. Guerard et al. Philadelphia: J. P. Lippincott Co., 1964. (Hawkes is one of the other editors)

69. The American Literary Anthology 1: the 1st Annual Collection of the Best from the Literary Magazines. Edited by John Hawkes et al. New York: Farrar, Straus & Giroux, 1968.

70. John Hawkes Reading at Stanford. [Sound Recording]. Stanford Program for Recordings in Sound, 1973. 1 disc CF-3164, 12 in., 33 1/3 rpm., mono., 55 min.

At a conference on "Myth Symbol Culture," sponsored by the graduate program in Modern Thought and Literature at Stanford University in 1972, Hawkes read selections from and offered comments on The Cannibal, Second Skin, The Blood Oranges, and his then forthcoming novel, Death, Sleep and the Traveler. This is a recording of Hawkes's reading, the second pressing of which (made in 1974) was still for sale by Serendipity Books Distribution in 1975 at a price of $7.00. Albert J. Guerard provides the notes on the record jacket.

71. [Letter to the Editor]. New York Times Book Review, May 5, 1974, p. 59.

Hawkes castigates David Bromwich for his "intolerable egoism" in tampering with Flannery O'Connor's admiration for The Lime Twig in his review of Death, Sleep and the Traveler (No. 345). The novelist declares that O'Connor possessed "clarity, precision, and strength of mind" and clearly liked The Lime Twig.

SEE ALSO: No. 595.

PART II

INTERVIEWS WITH HAWKES

72.   Beaumont, Julian.   "They're Trying to Create New
      Taste in Literature."   Boston Sunday Globe, June
      13, 1948. p. A-13.
      In a brief interview Hawkes, editor with Seymour
      Laurence and John Rogers of Wake, a literary maga-
      zine, and founder of the publication, explains the pur-
      pose of the magazine.

73.   Broussard, Ray.   "Novelist John Hawkes Visits Color-
      ado College to Participate in Current Festival of
      Fiction."   Colorado Springs Gazette-Telegraph,
      May 25, 1974, p. 12-D.
      This short interview presents Hawkes's comments
      on his own style and writings and offers a few com-
      ments on the novelist's past and present reputation.
      It affords the reader a quick impression of Hawkes's
      personality.

74.   Collins, Thomas.   "Spotlighting a 'Dark' Novelist."
      Garden City Newsday, October 25, 1971, p. 13-A.
      Includes several quotations derived from an inter-
      view with Hawkes concerning the novelist's technique,
      originality, purpose, fictive beginnings, and feelings
      about the Puritan ethic.   Collin's own comments con-
      centrate on Hawkes's recent arrival into the literary
      limelight, as well as on his poetic style and pleasant
      demeanor.   The interviewer also adds a few words on
      The Blood Oranges.

75.   Dolbier, Maurice.   "Puritan's Progress."   Washington
      Post, May 30, 1965, Book Week, p. 6.
      Obviously resulting from an interview with Hawkes,
      this article dwells largely on details of the novelist's
      career but offers statements by Hawkes on his style of

writing and on the lack of literary influences on his
work.   The closing Hawkesian quotation reads: "When
you write this, you can say that I'm a quiet and
friendly person, but be sure to add that as a writer
I'm cold and brutal. "

76.   Dunn, Douglas. "Profile 11: John Hawkes. " New
         Review 12 (March 1975): 23-8.
         Written after an interview with Hawkes, this ar-
ticle includes discussion of Hawkes's reputation and
method of and intentions in writing.   Dunn considers
Hawkes's originality and brilliance to be in his "creation of imaginative landscapes, " found most effectively in The Beetle Leg.   While Dunn underlines Hawkes's
aim to work "entirely through the imagination, " he
feels that Hawkes's most recent works lack the imaginative powers of the first novels and fears lest the
novelist's future works feature so much violence that
they become "subjectively unwholesome" and "objec-
tively contemptible. "

77.   Emerson, Paul.   "Author Adapts Skill as Novelist to
         Writing of Forceful Drama. "   Palo Alto Times,
         January 14, 1966, p. 11.
         In talking with Emerson just after the world pre-
miere of The Questions Hawkes briefly describes his
feelings in working with the Actor's workshop in San
Francisco.   Emerson explains how The Questions
came to be produced by Stanford Repertory Company.
Hawkes also reveals his aim in writing the plays: to
create a vision "based on the reality of the voices of
the characters and the dramatic action. "

78.   Enck, John.   "John Hawkes: an Interview. "   Wiscon-
         sin Studies in Comparative Literature 6 (Summer
         1965): 141-55; reprinted in The Contemporary
         Writer, pp. 3-17.   Edited by L. S. Dembo and
         Cyrena N. Pondrom.   Madison: University of
         Wisconsin Press, 1972; excerpted in The Merrill
         Studies in Second Skin, pp. 23-31 (No. 537).
         Valuable for an understanding of Hawkes's ideas
on the purpose of his writing and for his comments on
such writers as Céline, Henry James, William Faulkner, Flannery O'Connor, and Carson McCullers, as
well as on his own method of writing.   Much discussion also centers on The Lime Twig.   Hawkes's re-
sponses are fulsome.   Cited often in the critical literature.

79.   Fielding, Andrew. "John Hawkes Is a Very Nice Guy,
       and a Novelist of Sex and Death." Village Voice,
       May 24, 1976, pp. 45-7.
           Growing out of an interview with Hawkes, this
       article offers statements by the novelist concerning
       his estimation of his writing, fictive intent, percep-
       tion of reader appreciation of his works, advice to
       young writers, recollections of his early writing ca-
       reer, and feelings about his own personality. Inter-
       spersed among these comments are Fielding's re-
       marks about Hawkes's personal demeanor during the
       interview and while giving a class presentation, and
       about the writer's home surroundings. Also added are
       opinions of Hawkes by such noteworthies as Scholes,
       Guerard, Laughlin, and Baumbach, excerpts from re-
       reviews praising Hawkes, a short section from Kuehl's
       interview with Hawkes (No. 86), and passages from
       four of Hawkes's works. Most of the observations on
       Hawkes's personality and early career are seen here
       in print for the first time.

80.   Forrester, Viviane. "Entretien avec l'écrivain amér-
       icain John Hawkes." Le Monde (Paris), Febru-
       ary 15, 1974, pp. 13, 16.
           Revealed are various facts about Hawkes's up-
       bringing, education, activities, and purpose in writing
       fictional works. Allusions to some of Hawkes's nov-
       els are made. Particularly interesting and informa-
       tive is the closing statement by Hawkes: "Mon do-
       maine est celui de la compassion, des possibilités
       humaines illimitées et que l'on ne peut séparer d'une
       angoisse extrême. Mes romans sont vrais." (My
       domain is that of compassion, of limitless human pos-
       sibilities, and that which cannot be separated from
       extreme anguish. My novels ring true.)

81.   _____. "Le Prix du meilleur livre étranger à
       John Hawkes." La Quinzaine littéraire (Paris),
       February 16-28, 1974, pp. 3-4.
           In this conversation with Forrester, which took
       place around the time of Hawkes's receipt of the
       French Prize for the Best Foreign Book for 1973,
       Hawkes affirms once again that imagination as articu-
       lated through language is of utmost importance to him
       and emphasizes his constant attempt to reach the core
       of human possibility and dilemma. Forrester com-
       ments favorably on The Cannibal and The Blood Or-

anges and notes that both novels embody the essence
of our era.   Hawkes talks about The Cannibal and
Death, Sleep and the Traveler, calling the latter a
mythic vision of human life in its brevity and a clear,
brutal comedy which shows the ugliness within us, an
ugliness which, nonetheless, holds its own beauty.

82.   "Fruit Talks to John Hawkes."   Brown Daily Herald,
        April 25, 1974, Fresh Fruit Section, p. 3.
        In talking about fiction writing in the United States
and about his own work Hawkes asserts his interest
in fiction that "clearly defines itself as a product of
the imagination."   He also states his firm commit-
ment to teaching and denies a personal drive towards
"making it" as a writer.

83.   Graham, John.   "John Hawkes on His Novels: an In-
        terview with John Graham."   Massachusetts Re-
        view 7 (Summer 1966):   449-61; excerpted in The
        Merrill Studies in Second Skin, pp. 31-3 (No.
        537).
        An edited transcript of an unrehearsed discussion
between Hawkes and Professor Graham of the University of Virginia.   This interview was taped in April,
1965 for release in three fifteen-minute segments of
the "Scholar's Bookshelf," a radio program produced
by the Radio-Television Recording Center at the University of Virginia.   Cassette tape copies of the program segments are available from the Center at their
normal duplication fee.
        Frequently cited in the critical literature on
Hawkes, this discussion provides a lengthy look at
Hawkes's feelings about fiction writing and extended
treatments of various aspects of The Cannibal, The
Lime Twig, and Second Skin.

84.   Jaspersohn, William.   "An Interview with John
        Hawkes."   Bookletter 2 (February 2, 1976):   6-7.
        This November, 1975 interview covers several di-
verse topics.   Beginning with the more typical discussion of the way in which Hawkes began writing fiction
and how his novels, especially Death, Sleep and the
Traveler, originated, the conversation turns to such
subjects as the novelist's favorite writer (Barth), lesser known writers whom Hawkes knows and admires,
Hawkes's advice to younger writers, and, lastly, the
writer's reflections on his frustrated ambitions and
present wisdom in certain areas.

85.   Keyser, David and French, Ned. "Talks with John
       Hawkes." Harvard Advocate 104 (October 1970):
       6, 34-5.
       Recollecting his interview with the novelist, Key-
       ser dwells first on Hawkes's surprisingly mild appear-
       ance, then slightly on his war imagery, and, finally,
       on his attempt to "exorcise the devil out of life" in
       his works. He determines that Hawkes's terror and
       success lie in his forcing us to discover the terror
       that is latent within our world and within ourselves.
       French's reflections on his interview concern
       Hawkes's emphasis on language. He concludes that
       the creation of situations is more important to Hawkes
       than the situations themselves, and that we should
       thank Hawkes for seeing things through language that
       we should, but do not, see. French contends that the
       novelist is "refurbishing our language."

86.   Kuehl, John. "Interview." In his John Hawkes and
       the Craft of Conflict, pp. 155-83. New Brunswick,
       N.J.: Rutgers University Press, 1975.
       Touches upon many subjects pertaining to Hawkes
       and his work, ranging from Hawkes's intentions in
       writing novels ("to destroy conventional morality and
       conventional attitudes") to his thoughts on the applica-
       bility of the terms existentialist, surrealist, and anti-
       realist to himself. The conversation also turns to
       such topics as Christian allegory, ritual and myth in
       the novels and Hawkes's attitude towards religion,
       Hawkes's insistence upon the necessity of "reversed
       sympathy" to the novelistic experience, the conflict in
       Hawkes's novels between life and death forces, Hawkes's
       portrayal of children and of certain other characters,
       the novelist's definition of and use of comedy, and the
       language of Hawkes's fictions.

87.   Largillet, Jean-Pierre. "John Hawkes à la recherche
       de l'imagination." Nice-Matin, May 13, 1975, p.
       2.
       Affords the reader a glimpse of Hawkes's working
       and living habits while writing Travesty in Vence,
       France. Quotes Hawkes concerning his ambition to
       create a world of imagination in each of his works
       and the fact that each novel can be viewed both as
       nightmare and as love poetry.

88.   LaSusa, John. "An Interview with John Hawkes."

Footnotes 1.
Though very loosely-constructed this interview records Hawkes's explanation of why terror is a major
part of his work and his thoughts about the future of
the novel.

89.   MacBeth, George.   The Living Novelist: John
      Hawkes.   [Sound Recording]   British Broadcasting
      Corporation, 1975. 1 tape? 12 in. reels, 7-1/2
      ips., mono., 24 min. 49 sec.
      In this conversation, broadcast on the Third Pro-
gramme on September 1, 1975 from 8:55 to 9:25 P.M.,
MacBeth and Hawkes talk briefly about the common
themes of Hawkes's last three novels, the place of
eroticism in Hawkes's works, and the nature of the
narrator in Travesty (unpublished at the time). Most
importantly, Hawkes also outlines the action of Travesty and reads two lengthy passages from this novel--
the opening paragraphs and the section in which the
narrator imagines the death of the three main characters.
      No scripts of the tape are available for purchase
or loan.

90.   Pressman, Ailene S.   "John Hawkes, Author, Calls
      Guerard's Preface Most Helpful Ciriticism."
      Radcliffe News, March 17, 1950, pp. 2, 4.
      An extremely early interview which includes a
smattering of biographical material about the novelist
and some comments by Hawkes on his novel-in-prog-
ress, The Beetle Leg.

91.   Sauls, Roger.   "A Conversation with John Hawkes."
      Charlotte Observer, March 14, 1976, p. 10C.
      A handful of questions and answers touching main-
ly upon Faulkner's influence on Hawkes's works,
Hawkes's high regard for Flannery O'Connor's stories, the beginnings of Hawkes's writing career, and,
in fulsome terms, the purpose of fiction in Hawkes's
eyes.

92.   Scholes, Robert.   "A Conversation on The Blood Or-
      anges between John Hawkes and Robert Scholes."
      Novel 5 (Spring 1972): 197-207; reprinted in The
      New Fiction: Interviews with Innovative American
      Writers, pp. 97-112.   Edited by Joe David Bella-
      my.   London: University of Illinois Press, 1974.

In their talk Hawkes and Scholes, a noted critic
of modern fiction, focus on The Blood Oranges, as
the title suggests. Hawkes not only maintains that
the novel is about the imagination and about sexuality,
but also that its ideas of "sexual extention ...
are meant to test our language, ourselves, our illusory
existence" and should not be thought of in terms of
"wife-swapping. " He further discusses the four main
characters of the novel, some of the images, the Illyrian setting, and the origins of the book. Throughout the conversation Hawkes also responds to questions about and offers statements concerning his fiction as a whole, his theory of fiction, and the purpose of fiction, with a few additional thoughts on the
power of the "great arts of the imagination" and on
optimism and pessimism as outlooks on life.

SEE ALSO: Nos. 61, 371-3, 396, 600.

PART III

BIOGRAPHICAL MATERIAL ON HAWKES

93.   "Books-Authors." New York Times, February 2,
       1965, p. 30.
       Names Hawkes's Second Skin as a contender for
       the National Book Award in fiction for 1964 along with
       the novels of six other authors, including Saul Bellow,
       Vladimir Nabokov, and Isaac B. Singer.

94.   "Brown Professor Given $10,500 Fellowship." Provi-
       dence Evening Bulletin, September 16, 1963, p.
       22.
       Hawkes's receipt of the Ford Foundation Fellow-
       ship to study "stage problems and dramatic writing
       for a year" is reported. The Guggenheim and Nation-
       al Institute awards of the previous year are men-
       tioned, as well as the upcoming publications of Second
       Skin in January, 1964.

95.   Cohn, Ruby. "Hawkes, John (Clendennin Burne, Jr.)."
       In Contemporary Dramatists, pp. 358-60. Edited
       by James Vinson. New York: St. Martin's
       Press, 1973.
       Personal and career dates through 1968, a bibliog-
       raphy of Hawkes's major works through 1971, and
       three critical studies of Hawkes are listed. Also
       found here are a statement by the novelist on his rea-
       son for writing his plays and a brief description of
       each play with some analysis by Cohn.

96.   Directory of American Scholars, 6th ed. S. v.
       "Hawkes, John C. B. Jr."
       Gives unannotated biographical facts through 1974.

97.   "Dulce Est Periculum." Harvard Advocate 133 (De-
       cember 1949): 2-3.
       Announces Charivari's publication as imminent

and mentions Hawkes's diligence in his work at the
Harvard University Press.

98.   "18 Grants of $2,000 Awarded by Institute of Arts and
        Letters." New York Times, May 4, 1962, p. 22.
        Discloses that Hawkes is among the eighteen
        writers, artists, and composers receiving grants from
        the National Institute of Arts and Letters.

99.   "15 Writers Given Theater Grants." New York Times,
        September 16, 1963, p. 44-L.
        Hawkes is cited as one of fifteen writers who re-
        ceived a 1964-65 Ford Foundation Fellowship.   The
        article provides an explanation of the fellowship pro-
        gram and its purpose and names all of the year's re-
        cipients.

100.   Frankel, Haskell. "On the Fringe: Professor to
        Ping Pong Players." Saturday Review, July 25,
        1964, pp. 22-3.
        Includes several remarks by Hawkes concerning
        his home, family, and students.

101.   Gaiser, Carolyn. "Voices on the Mountain; Writers
        at Sea." Glamour, May 1964, pp. 54, 56, 86,
        88, 90, 98. [90, 98]
        In a few sentences Hawkes's success at the Bread
        Loaf Writers' Conference is noted.   Hawkes is dubbed
        an "astute critic," an inspiration to all because of the
        "intensity of his perception," and a defendant of the
        "consciousness closed in on itself."

102.   Guerard, Albert J. "John Hawkes in English J."
        Harvard Advocate 104 (October 1970): 10-11.
        A glimpse of Hawkes as a student in Guerard's
        classes and in the years immediately following Hawkes's
        graduation.

103.   "Guggenheim Foundation Awards Stipends to Twelve
        Faculty Members for 1962-63." Brown Daily
        Herald, April 30, 1962, pp. 1, 4.
        Along with eleven other faculty members at Brown
        University Hawkes is named as a recipient of a Gug-
        genheim award.   The article states that Hawkes was
        intending to use the award to work on a novel some-
        where in the British West Indies.

104. "Hawkes, John (Clendennin Burne, Jr.) 1925- ."
     In Contemporary Authors; a Bio-bibliographical
     Guide to Current Authors and Their Work, vol. 1,
     p. 432. 1st revision. Edited by James M. Eth-
     ridge and Barbara Kopala. Detroit: Gale Re-
     search Co., 1967.
     Offers personal and career data through 1965, ex-
     cerpts from remarks by Trachtenberg, Galloway, Fro-
     hock, Charles Matthews, and Guerard about Hawkes's
     work, and a selected list of biographical and critical
     sources on Hawkes.

105. "Hawkes, John (Clendennin Burne, Jr.)." In Contem-
     porary Novelists, pp. 570-3. Edited by James
     Vinson. London, New York: St. Martin's Press,
     1972.
     A good, short introduction to Hawkes and his writ-
     ings. Provides unannotated biographical facts through
     1966, a list of publications (mainly of Hawkes's major
     works), an excerpt from Enck's interview with the nov-
     elist (No. 78) concerning his fictive aim, and a lengthy
     estimate of Hawkes's work by Albert Guerard.

106. "Hawkes Awarded Ford Fellowship." Brown Daily
     Herald, September 17, 1963, p. 1.
     An abbreviated version of the Providence Evening
     Bulletin's article (No. 94) on Hawkes's Ford Founda-
     tion Fellowship.

107. "Hawkes to Receive Grant from Institute to Write a
     Novel." Brown Daily Herald, May 7, 1962, p. 1.
     Hawkes's $2,000 grant from the National Institute
     of Arts and Letters is proclaimed. The novelist's in-
     tention to use this money to finance work on his next
     novel during the 1962-63 academic year while situated
     in the British West Indies is also included. In addi-
     tion, found here are a few quotations from an unnamed
     reviewer's comments about Hawkes's meritorious "vi-
     sionary" novels, and one by Hawkes on his reason for
     using nightmare and horror in his works.

108. Howard, Lawrence M. "Brown Novelist Gets Subsi-
     dies." Providence Sunday Journal, May 6, 1962,
     p. N-33.
     Tells of the Guggenheim award and the National
     Institute of Arts and Letters grant to Hawkes. Gives,
     too, a few words about Hawkes's early writing career

and some comments by the novelist about his work.

109.   The International Who's Who, 1974-75, 38th ed.   S.v.
       "Hawkes, John."
           Cites concisely details of Hawkes's personal back-
       ground and career achievements.   Notes the author's
       published major works through Death, Sleep and the
       Traveler.

110.   "John Hawkes."   In Cyclopedia of World Authors, vol.
       2, pp. 803-5.   Rev. ed.   Edited by Frank North-
       ern Magill.   Englewood Cliffs, N.J.:   Salem
       Press, 1974.
           Hawkes's background and achievements through
       1965 are given in essay form.   Added also are a few
       comments on Hawkes's reputation, style, and aim in
       writing.   One factual error is noted: Hawkes's date
       of marriage was September 5, 1947, not 1957.

111.   "New Writers' Workshop to Bring Authors Here."
       Aspen Times, May 25, 1962, p. 1.
           Among other well-known writers such as Jan de
       Hartog and Kenneth Rexroth, Hawkes is cited as about
       to take part in a writers' workshop sponsored by the
       Aspen Institute in Aspen, Colorado during the summer
       of 1962 from June 24th to July 7th.

112.   Pocalyko, Michael.   "John Hawkes Literary Sympos-
       ium Highlights Muhlenberg Arts Festival."   Muhl-
       enberg Weekly Festival Edition (Allentown, Pa.),
       March 22, 1976, pp. 2-3.
           Furnishes advanced notice of the two-day John
       Hawkes Symposium at Muhlenberg College on April 9
       and 10, 1976.   Hawkes, "a major writer and the man
       who is perhaps America's most successful innovator in
       the novel form," is said to be attending and reading
       from his works.   Pertinent career information is given
       about the thirteen American scholars who would be
       gathering at the Symposium to offer critical interpre-
       tations of Hawkes's writing.   James Laughlin, Hawkes's
       American publisher, is also noted as an attendee.

113.   "Prominent Writers to Speak at College."   Colorado
       Springs Gazette-Telegraph, May 5, 1974, p. 6-A.
           Announces an upcoming fiction festival at Colorado
       College, during which Hawkes, winner of three major
       awards, is stated to be scheduled to speak.

114. The Reader's Adviser; a Layman's Guide to Litera-
     ture, 12th ed. S. v. "Hawkes, John, 1925- ."
     A few paragraphs of comments largely on The
     Lime Twig, Second Skin, and The Blood Oranges with
     extensive quotes from reviews by Webster Schott and
     Santha Rama Ran. Basic biographical facts are
     stated, accompanied by a very short bibliography.

115. "Three Editors Bring Out New Wake." Harvard Crim-
     son, May 7, 1948, p. 2.
     Documents the fact that Hawkes was the founder
     of the literary magazine, Wake, at Harvard. At this
     date the magazine was offering its sixth issue.

116. "Two R. I. Natives, Brown Man Win $2,000 Literary
     Grants." Providence Journal, May 4, 1962, p. 7.
     The National Institute of Arts and Letters awards
     to John Hawkes, Edwin O'Connor, and Galway Kinnell
     are highlighted in this article about all of the 1962 re-
     cipients of the grants. Mentioned in the few sentences
     about Hawkes are four of his novels.

117. Ullyot, James R. and Paisner, Bruce L. "Counsel
     for Grove Press Defends Miller's Novel." Har-
     vard Crimson, December 12, 1961, p. 1.
     At a Winthrop House Forum at Harvard Hawkes
     defends Tropic of Cancer as an important influence
     on the contemporary American novel but finds that the
     book is not obscene enough and is to be criticized for
     its partially anti-homosexual stance.

118. Van Dusen, Bruce B. "716 Students Get Brown De-
     grees." Providence Evening Bulletin, June 4,
     1962, p. 1, 19. [19]
     In relating the details of Brown University's 194th
     commencement names Hawkes as one of the recipi-
     ent's of a Master of Arts ad Eundem.

119. Who's Who in America, 1974/75, 38th ed. S. v.
     "Hawkes, John."
     Personal, school, and career information are
     listed without elaboration. Contains more details than
     No. 109.

120. Who's Who in the East, 1974/75, 14th ed. S. v.
     "Hawkes, John."

Offers the same information as No. 119 with the
exception that The Blood Oranges is the latest novel
noted.

121.   Who's Who in the World, 1974-75, 2nd ed.   S. v.
       "Hawkes, John."
       The same in content as No. 120.

122.   World Authors, 1950-1970; a Companion Volume to
       Twentieth Century Authors.   S. v.   "Hawkes,
       John (Clendennin Burne)."
       Beginning with a short account by Hawkes of his
       life, emphasizing the places in which he has lived and
       how they affected him, the article continues with com-
       ments about each of Hawkes's major works through
       The Blood Oranges.   Remarks by a few reviewers and
       critics are included.   Concluding statements concern
       Hawkes's teaching and writing career and precede a
       selected bibliography on Hawkes.

123.   "Writers' Conference."   Boston Sunday Herald, May
       21, 1961, p. 22.
       A three-picture photographic treatment of the Bos-
       ton College Writers' Conference.   In one of the photos
       Hawkes, who attended the Conference to take part in a
       panel discussion on fiction, is seen talking with Rev.
       John A. O'Callaghan, S.J., Professor of English at
       Boston College.

SEE ALSO: Nos. 72-5, 78-80, 82-7, 90-2, 574, 650.

PART IV

REVIEWS OF HAWKES'S WORKS

A. NOVELS

Charivari

124. "Old Directions." Time, January 16, 1950, pp. 98-
      9. [99]
         An article about New Directions 11 and Laughlin
      which spends a few phrases on "the Harvard student
      John Hawkes," who like some other new writers
      in the anthology, loses his "story in a messy Joycean
      montage of elliptical dialogue and overfertilized imag-
      ery."

SEE ALSO: Nos. 317, 449-50, 454-6, 458-9, 464-6.

The Cannibal

125. "Books Briefly Noted." New Yorker, January 28,
      1950, p. 85.
         "Mr. Hawkes' writing is cold, brilliant, and cryp-
      tic," and his present novel is "a pointed account of
      life among the defeated."

126. Bradbury, Malcolm. "New Fiction." Punch, March
      27, 1963, pp. 461-2. [462] o
         Totally favorable in its content, considers the nov-
      el a "remarkable evocation of the crisis of European
      history in the past fifty years" and deserving of much
      more attention than it has received.

127. Bush, Douglas. "American Writers Come Back from
      the Wars." New Republic, October 30, 1950, pp.
      21-4. [23]
         In a passing allusion to this novel Bush calls it a

"brilliant nightmare, where war is the indistinct background, or most violent expression, of the inner crav-
ings and tensions of modern man. "

128.   Clowes, John. "Attention Please, Aficionados: This
        May Well Be a Milestone. " Louisville Courier-
        Journal, March 12, 1950, sec. 3, p. 19. o
        A satirical review which calls on "aficionados" to
judge whether or not this work is "another milestone
on the road to ultimate art" and laughingly indicates
that the reviewer couldn't understand the novel.

129.   Coleman, S. H. "The Cannibal, by John Hawkes. "
        Chicago Review 4 (Winter 1950): 44-5. +
        A political interpretation of the novel is attempted,
although, in general, the book is described as confusing and difficult to understand. So too, the novel is
pronounced "impressive, stimulating and very moving, "
with vividly depicted characters and incidents. Coleman further states: "The style is remarkable for a
writer of Hawkes' comparative inexperience... "

130.   Cranston, Maurice. Review of The Cannibal. London
        Magazine n. s. 8 (February 1969): 95-6. o
        Among the numerous laudatory phrases sprinkled
throughout this review are statements comparing
Hawkes to Kafka and Djuna Barnes. The novel is
called "uncompromisingly highbrow, " whose theme
"should be understood as the whole drama of the German soul since its emergence in the nineteenth century. "

131.   Davis, Robert Gorham. "Fiction Chronicle. " Parti-
        san Review 17 (May-June 1950): 519-23. [522]
        o
        This novel portrays the ruined cities of Germany
more imaginatively in one paragraph than all of John
Hersey's The Wall manages to do. Yet Hawkes's vision is really so alien to our normal experience that
the reader cannot grasp it readily.

132.   Elliott, Janice. "Ice-cold. " New Statesman, October
        25, 1968, pp. 552-3. [522] -
        "For all his obscurities, he [Hawkes] uses lan-
guage and imagery with such hypnotic power that if
you can take him at all, you are engulfed to the point
where plot and meaning seem almost immaterial. "

Hawkes treats his reader harshly, though, since he "writes as if in a fearful, visionary dream and forces you to share that dream. "

133. Engle, Paul. " 'Pleasurable Terror' from a First Novel. " Chicago Sunday Tribune Magazine of Books, February 19, 1950, p. 5. -
"One of the most brilliant first books to be published in this country in a long time, " says Engle, admiring Hawkes's rhythmic prose, imaginative phrasing, and rich detail. He notes further that the novel moves by means of "abrupt flashes of insight, " which provide the story with tension, and that the terror found in the book is "that pleasurable terror which belongs to art. "

134. Flint, F. Cudworth. "Nine First Novels. " Sewanee Review 59 (Winter 1951): 137-51. [145-6] +
Naming the novel a "twentieth-century City of Dreadful Night, " Flint considers it "essentially a poetic evocation: a vision of despair, " which captures perfectly his memory of the postwar eeriness of a devastated Germany.

135. Forrester, Viviane. "Une sauvage originalité. " La Quinzaine littéraire (Paris), June 16-30, 1972, pp. 3-4; reprinted in L'Année littéraire 1972: Choix d'articles publiés par "La Quinzaine littéraire, " pp. 85-7. Présenté par Maurice Nadeau. Paris: La Quinzaine littéraire, 1973. +
Assures the reader in highly literary terms that the novel is concerned with our times and occupied Germany, that it tells us about ordinary existence in disguise, and does so with "une rare, insolite liberté des images et des investissements" (a rare, unaccustomed freedom of images and symbols). Calls The Cannibal one of the major novels of our times--one that is full of depth and "sauvage originalité" (savage originality).

136. H(arrop), M(ona). Review of The Cannibal. Cincinnati Times-Star, February 18, 1950, p. 9.
Readers of this "tale of a fantastic and hallucinated Germany between 1919 and 1945" may recall with pride ten years from now that they were among the first to recognize Hawkes's unique, perhaps major, talent.

137.   Howe, Irving. "The Novel in Mid-Century." <u>Report-</u>
       <u>er</u>, December 26, 1950, pp. 35-8. [38]
       "An arresting novel of postwar Germany" and "one
       of the few recent novels that seem intimately related
       to our experience as we immediately know it."

138.   J(ones), C(arter) B(rooke). Review of <u>The Cannibal.</u>
       <u>Washington Sunday Star,</u> February 12, 1950, sec.
       C. p. 3. o
       The book contains some "extraordinarily vivid de-
       scriptions" and, no doubt, is as surrealistic, symbol-
       ic, and allegorical as Albert Guerard assesses. How-
       ever, "why write a novel that requires a key and a
       compass?"

139.   K., A. "Among the New Books." <u>San Francisco</u>
       <u>Sunday Chronicle,</u> May 28, 1950, <u>This World</u> sec-
       tion, p. 22. o
       Reading this novel is like "going through a long
       nightmare, one that is not exactly understood in the
       light of day, but which leaves you disturbed and slight-
       ly shaken."

140.   Klein, Alexander. "The Merely New." <u>New Repub-</u>
       <u>lic,</u> March 27, 1950, p. 20. +
       An uncomplimentary piece which nearly charges
       Hawkes and his publisher with merely trying to be
       different by stressing "newness" in this novel, rather
       than concentrating on its "specific direction and
       achievement." Castigating the novelist's lack of con-
       cern for "people, emotions, character" and his inat-
       tention to selectivity, the reviewer generally feels that
       Hawkes "manages for long stretches to make dullness
       and surrealism appear practically synonymous."

141.   Mandel, Paul W. "To Skin a Fox." <u>Harvard Crim-</u>
       <u>son</u>, February 23, 1950, p. 3. -
       Sees this "intense and confusing book" to be pre-
       occupied with decay, disgust, and "the warriors and
       valkyries of the German folk-myths." Nonetheless,
       accords much praise to Hawkes for his style and ef-
       fective "wallowing" in the "racial unconscious."

142.   Markfield, Wallace. "Three First Novels." <u>Com-</u>
       <u>mentary</u>, April 1950, pp. 390-2. [391-2] +
       Hawkes is a "cold and brilliant writer," who,
       though obsessed with filth and decay, has a "superb

eye for visual and olfactory detail. " He attempts to
"portray obsessions of many different minds submerged
in a nightmare, " and manages to capture what others,
writing in the Kafkaesque way, have not: "the achievement of truth through distortion. "

143. Nye, Robert. "Degrees of Urgency. " Manchester
Guardian, November 8, 1968, p. 8. o
The highest accolades are accorded here as The
Cannibal is called "the best American novel to have
come out of the Second World War. " "A mad, difficult, gruesome, and disaster-ridden book; it may be
a great one. " Further, the novel is seen to show
"the pitiful absolute sense of a world at war with itself for the second time" and the enactment of the
"double dislocation of everything" in yet another dislo-
cating factor: that of language.

144. "Other New Novels. " Times Literary Supplement,
March 22, 1963, p. 205.
Considers this novel to be a "surrealist nightmare
about ruin, " which has all of the despair found in
Borchert's Draussen vor der Tür but none of the com-
passion.

145. Parone, Edward. "The Macabre Mice. " Hartford
Courant, March 12, 1950, Magazine Section, p.
15. +
Parone renders moderate praise as he prophesies
that Hawkes's novel will not be widely read because of
its obscurity; he acknowledges the "considerable worth"
of the book, which "saves us from cliché, " and adds
that "the illusion of a world on the edge of insanity is
communicated by a prose on the edge of the same region. "

146. Redman, Ben Ray. "German Degeneration & Collapse. " Saturday Review, March 11, 1950, p. 16-
7; excerpted in Modern American Literature, p.
49 (No. 587). +
One of the lengthiest reviews on The Cannibal,
this piece focuses on Hawkes's striking imagery, verbal skill, and resourcefulness. Redman agrees with
Guerard's estimation of Hawkes as more difficult than
either Faulkner or Kafka in that Hawkes's "imagination
is a more undisciplined force than Faulkner's" and
that, unlike Kafka, Hawkes "sacrifices the whole to

the part. " Yet his overriding feeling is that the novel,
as a whole, is "less than comprehensible" and that
the novelist's future success will depend on his attainment of some self-discipline in his writing.

147.   Review of The Cannibal.   Christian Science Monitor.
            February 18, 1950, Magazine Section, p. 4.
        "A dispassionately macabre allegory of modern
        Germany and, indirectly, of modern civilization... "

148.   Review of The Cannibal.   Kirkus 18 (January 15,
            1950): 38. o
        "A revelation of the soul of Germany ... through
        an intense vision of horror. " Requires, despite its
        brilliant descriptions, a "calm center of sustained at-
        tention" to transform this from a confusing into a
        compelling novel.

149.   Review of The Cannibal.   St. Louis Star-Times,
            April 12, 1950, p. 25.
        "A sort of allegory of Germany, " which is fasci-
        nating and compelling, although it is anybody's guess
        as to what it signifies.

150.   Review of The Cannibal.   United States Quarterly
            Book Review 6 (June 1950): 157-8. o
        Hawkes is a "young writer of extraordinary gifts, "
        who has succeeded in creating a work utilizing com-
        plex symbols, "intended to illuminate the forces oper-
        ative in Germany in two periods of crisis, " and re-
        quiring much close interpretation to determine the apt-
        ness of the symbolism.

151.   Rogers, John.   "The Cannibal by John Hawkes. "
            Harvard Advocate 133 (March 1950): 12, 19-20.
            *
        A deep, critical analysis, presenting some of the
        scenes and characters of the novel and praising
        Hawkes for his "special configuration of a dying polit-
        ical and historical genus, a sometimes neologistic re-
        alignment of figure and fantasy to produce something
        not touched upon before--the echoes of war, fate, and
        myth in so many lives. "

152.   S. , A. V.   "Unique, Cold Novel. "   New Haven Regis-
            ter, February 19, 1950, Magazine Section, p. 10.
            +

Denying the difficulty of the novel, admires
Hawkes's inventiveness and ingenuity in creating a
"kind of German 'Wasteland'," where the picture of
modern Germany is given in nightmarish, surreal images. Dislikes, however, Hawkes's "cold scientific
precision" and the novel's "deliberate absence of a
feeling of sympathy for any of the characters."

153. Seymour-Smith, Martin. "Fiction of the Week: Hu-
      manity's Frightening Quality." Oxford (England)
      Mail, October 24, 1968, p. 10.
      "One of the most original books of the century,"
this novel, both weird and powerful, is worthy of being reread at intervals. "Hawkes is one of the first
'anti-realists'."

154. "Teutonic Nightmare." Time, February 6, 1950, 90,
      92. -
      This is a "dizzying surrealistic vision of postwar
Germany," in which, surprisingly enough, Hawkes
feels that he is telling "a perfectly straight story."

155. Wiener, Max. "World of Madness." Newark Sunday
      News, June 18, 1950, sec. 3, p. 50. -
      Proclaims Hawkes to be a "genuine talent" but
echoes Redman's feeling that the novelist must introduce discipline and clarity into his writing to attract
a larger audience. Says Wiener, in a positive tone:
"Mere realism, no matter how unblinking, is reduced
to Pollyana dimensions by comparison with the savage,
skilled heightening of stench and madness which this
author achieves."

156. "The Year in Books." Time, December 18, 1950,
      99-100, 102-7. [105]
      In one sentence characterizes this as a "some-
times powerful experimental novel that tried to capture the nightmarish quality of Germany's disintegra-
tion in defeat."

SEE ALSO: Nos. 183, 220, 223, 235, 250, 292.

                        The Beetle Leg

157. C., E. "Surrealist Subjects Time to Family Tale."
      Hartford Times, December 1, 1951, p. 18.

"A strange and pseudo-mythical tale of an extraordinary family," which is fascinating for the avant-
garde specialist.

158.   Creeley, Robert. "How to Write a Novel." New
       Mexico Quarterly 22 (Summer 1952): 239-41.
       [41]
       Creeley talks mainly of the traditional purpose and
       use of time in novels. In his final sentences, he
       notes that "the present novel" (The Beetle Leg) is in-
       teresting because it is aimed at bringing "time back to
       a use which isn't crippling."

159.   Edlin, Joseph J. "Heavy with Symbolism." St. Louis
       Post-Dispatch, April 4, 1952, p. 2C.   o
       Symbolism pervades this novel, which bears the
       unmistakable influence of James Joyce. For, like
       Joyce, Hawkes's "obsession with death gradually yields
       to a new concern with life." Yet, the poetic narration
       and symbolistic psychology become so involved that the
       novel is much like a modern abstract painting and can
       mean "many things to many people."

160.   Elliott, Janice. "The Bones of the West." Times
       (London), December 2, 1967, p. 22.   +
       While enjoying the language ("flowering but never
       flowery") and the use of classical myths in this book,
       prefers Second Skin to it. Feels that The Beetle Leg
       has been so compressed and pared down to the "bare
       bone of truth" that it is obscure and fails to communi-
       cate.

161.   Flint, F. Cudworth. "Fiction Chronicle." Sewanee
       Review 60 (October-December 1952): 706-21.
       [713-4] o
       Flint confesses his inability to understand the nov-
       el, whose point of reference has been engulfed by the
       nightmare scene, in his estimation. He does see
       the book, though, as a "rather Cocteau-ish miscellany."

162.   Guerard, Albert J. "Some Recent Novels." Perspec-
       tives, U.S.A., No. 1 (Fall 1952), pp. 168-72.
       [170-1] o
       Wonders about the obscurity of some passages but
       praises Hawkes's "saving stylistic drive and inventive-
       ness" and a verbal power which even Nathanael West
       lacked.

163. Haltrecht, Montague. "Institutionalised." <u>Sunday</u>
     <u>Times</u> (London), December 17, 1967, p. 26. o
     An antagonistic piece, in which Haltrecht admits
     his bafflement at the novel's meaning and cries out:
     "Mr. Hawkes's exuding egocentricity makes me want
     to beat my puny fists against his ivory tower, if not
     actually to put dynamite under it."

164. Hollander, J. "Improvised Alibis." <u>Listener,</u> July
     18, 1968, pp. 85-6. +
     Reviews three of Hawkes's works and finds that
     in each the protagonists are "ambiguously picaresque"
     and the style "darkly idiosyncratic." Considers <u>The</u>
     <u>Beetle Leg</u> annoying because of its "impenetrable syn-
     tax, factitious vernacular speech, overt referential
     solecism," and <u>The Innocent Party,</u> the least success-
     ful of Hawkes's plays, full of dialogue that will quick-
     ly fade from memory. Finds in <u>The Lime Twig,</u>
     though, stylistic and imaginative advances not in the
     other two works treated, and a measure of success
     owing to the purging power of its "violence and anti-
     suspense plot."

165. K(err), G(ilbert). Review of <u>The Beetle Leg.</u> Har-
     vard Advocate 135 (December 1951): 26-8. *
     Compared with <u>The Cannibal</u>, this new novel is
     richer in its language and has a more complex "inter-
     play of feeling." It possesses characters which are
     "both evanescent and omnipresent, haunting the situa-
     tion rather than dwelling in it," along with "subtly ex-
     aggerative distortion" and dark imagery. A powerful-
     ly written book, it requires concentration to read and
     is truly something new and different in the world of
     the novel.

166. L., E. A. "An American Love Story." <u>Boston Sun-</u>
     day Globe, December 9, 1951, p. 14-B. o
     Hawkes blends poetic thought with cryptic prose,
     "a mixture of myth and realism, symbolical and sad."
     Anyone who likes obscure puzzles will like the book.

167. McCaig, Helen. "New Novel on Hall Library Reserve
     Shelf Reaches High in Obscurity of Plot." <u>Gaines-</u>
     <u>ville</u> (Georgia) <u>Times</u>, January 6, 1952, p. 8. +
     Warns the reader that effort is needed in reading
     this novel because of the lack both of a straight story
     and of a sympathetic portrayal of characters and also

because of the great attention to detail. Finds that,
though it is not as good as The Cannibal, it offers "a
communication of honor, of amorality, of the wither-
ing away of human spirit," and is rewarding in detail,
if not in story.

168.   Pearson, Craig M. "Nightmare Theme." Hartford
        Courant, December 16, 1951, Magazine section,
        p. 18. -
        Through selected quotations from the novel and
short descriptions of the characters Pearson provides
a glimpse of Hawkes's landscape, a "land with the awful feeling that a man smothered in the mud has some-
how precluded violence and death." He considers
Hawkes to be a "young and daring innovator," whose
greatness can be seen on the horizon in view of the
novelist's "successive attempts with uncharted rhythms
of communication."

169.   Pfaff, William. Review of The Beetle Leg. Com-
        monweal, January 25, 1952, p. 407; excerpted in
        Modern American Literature, pp. 49-50 (No. 587).
        o
        Hawkes is an unusually talented writer, who packs
his sentences with poetic detail but overworks both the
use of detail and that of stylistic devices. The characters are overwrought and "are destroyed when looked
at from outside of Mr. Hawkes' intense, very private
world."

170.   Phelps, Robert. "Fiction Parade." New Republic,
        February 18, 1952, p. 21. o
        While feeling that Hawkes has a "keen sense of the
word," finds no communication of "felt experience" in
the novel and notices perfunctory "New Directions man-
nerisms."

171.   Politzer, Heinz. "Five Novels." Commentary, May
        1952, 510-2, 514. [514] -
        "Hawkes deals with the American experience of
Europe," as he brings to his novel the atmosphere of
postwar Europe. Stylistic experiment, an attempt at
"artistic integrity in the avant-garde tradition," and
blurred narrative are all here. But also there is
"fresh air and a savage beauty that verges on the archaic and the primitive."

172.   Raynolds, Robert. "Landscape in Purgatory." New
          York Times Book Review, December 30, 1951,
          p. 12. o
          Criticizes the novelist for his attempt at impress-
          ing his readers with "vivid imagery," rather than
          communicating with them. Adds that the novel "is
          more like a retrogression from poetry than an advance
          in the novel," since it does not have the "ordered in-
          tensity of a lyric poem" and is not "grown-up" enough
          to be a novel.

173.   Review of The Beetle Leg. Louisville Courier-Jour-
          nal, March 2, 1952, sec. 3, p. 10.
          "Even more irritating than its title," this is a
          novel in which "everything is in an arty, rhythmic
          monotone that doesn't quite come to life--or even make
          sense."

174.   Review of The Beetle Leg. New Yorker, January 12,
          1952, p. 74.
          While this novel has some extraordinary scenes,
          time after time the story appears to break off into a
          "series of keen but unrelated images," and the result
          is "only a tangle of inflexible, pampered wisps of
          writing."

175.   Review of The Beetle Leg, [by Edward J. Fitzgerald].
          Saturday Review, February 9, 1952, p. 35.
          Mr. Hawkes apparently is aiming at "a sort of
          myth (in the James Joyce sense) which incorporates all
          the standard paraphernalia of the Western story and
          invests it with legendary meaning." Unfortunately,
          his "turgid prose" leads the reader to lose his way
          and his interest.

176.   "Surrealist Western." Newsweek, December 31, 1951,
          pp. 58-9. -
          Cautiously explains the structure of the novel.
          Yet acknowledges that "Hawkes's imagination and graph-
          ic powers are so unusual" and the effect of adding
          elements of a Western so incongruous that the pattern
          of The Beetle Leg is like that of no other novel.

177.   Szanto, George. "Innocence and Relationship." Cath-
          olic World, February 28, 1968, pp. 237-8. +
          Covering The Beetle Leg and The Innocent Party,
          designates the former as a "difficult novel" and the

latter as plays which are "sexually dominated." In
both works Szanto detects a tension in the "subsurface
forward movement," promoted by Hawkes's tendency
never to state but continually to suggest action.

178.   W., L. B. "No 'New Direction' Seen by Reviewer in
        'The Beetle'." Pasadena Star-News, January 6,
        1952, p. 37. o
        After reading this novel, in which we could under-
        stand very little of the plot, we have come to the
        conclusion that "this is the poorest excuse for a nov-
        el that we have read in a long time."

179.   Wall, Stephen.   "Landscape with Figures." Observer
        (London), December 10, 1967, p. 28. -
        While asserting that this novel should rely less
        on Hawkes's intense prose power and that sometimes
        the novelist applies "verbal concentration" in an "in-
        discriminate manner," the reviewer lauds Hawkes's
        style as holding "exceptional promise."

SEE ALSO: Nos. 183, 223, 250, 334, 368.

                    The Goose on the Grave

180.   Dickey, James L.   "Verve and Invention in Hawkes'
        Two Novels."   Houston Post, June 5, 1954, sec.
        5, p. 4. +
        Dickey states that this third work by Hawkes
        "displays more inventiveness, more verve, a sharper
        and more compelling narrative drive than could be
        culled from the entire output of the American writers
        his age." Nonetheless, he is disappointed in the
        book's title novel, and notes that, in general, Hawkes's
        stories lack coherence and emanate in each instance
        "a clouded brightness of unease, impossible finally to
        assimilate."

181.   Leigh, Michael.   Review of The Goose on the Grave
        and The Owl.   Pensacola News-Journal, June 6,
        1954, sec. 2, p. 4.
        Both of these stories, long to be remembered,
        "strike a valid though discordant note." They are by
        a writer whose talent is "haunting, elusive and more
        than a little macabre."

182. M., A. Review of The Goose on the Grave and The
        Owl. Black Mountain Review 1, no. 1 (1954):
        58-9. -
        The Owl, a dream-structure which, of the two
      novels seen here, best displays Hawkes's world of
      "deep and careful terror." It is an allegory, like
      most of Hawkes's works, and presents "characters,
      virtues, and vices ... which are met with in the
      old Morality Plays."

183. Mercier, Vivian. "Moyenageux." Commonweal,
        July 2, 1954, p. 323; excerpted in Modern Amer-
        ican Literature, p. 50 (No. 587). +
        Both The Owl and The Goose on the Grave are
      far less successful than The Beetle Leg, which, in it-
      self, is a vast improvement over The Cannibal. The
      Beetle Leg "has some of Al Capp's grotesque, wry
      humor," is written in a plausible vernacular, con-
      tains all the necessary information about its charac-
      ters, and offers a story worth knowing. On the con-
      trary, The Owl, whose allegorical meaning still
      eludes me, has a "phony medievalism" and "is un-
      done by its rhetoric," while The Goose on the Grave
      appears to lack some necessary information and in-
      furiatingly escapes me even on the literal level.

184. Review of The Goose on the Grave. Louisville Cour-
        ier-Journal, June 20, 1954, sec. 3, p. 9.
        The novels are difficult to follow but have de-
      scriptions which are "nearly always poetic, richly dec-
      orative, and satisfyingly evocative of both the sinister
      and beautiful in Mr. Hawkes' Italian settings."

185. Review of The Goose on the Grave. Virginia Quarter-
        ly Review, 30 (Autumn 1954): xcii.
        "These two short novels are a kind of baroque
      Kafka performance set in Italy." However, while
      Kafka's novels have lucid surfaces but obscure mean-
      ings, Hawkes's "are obscure in both surface and
      meaning."

186. Quinn, Patrick F. "Fiction Chronicle." Hudson Re-
        view 7 (Autumn 1954): 460-5. [464]
        In talking of works by Céline and Toynbee, as
      well as of Hawkes's Goose on the Grave, feels that
      all three are "gimmicky" and that "one can barely
      summon the energy needed to read them." Agreeing

with Mercier's comments on Hawkes's work (See No.
183), describes the book as a "dogged experimental
effort."

187.   Stone, Jerome.   "Surrealistic Threesome." Saturday
       Review, July 24, 1954, pp. 35-6; excerpted in
       Modern American Literature, p. 50 (No. 587). o
       Calls Hawkes's writing "oracular, cryptic, and
       cold" but finds these two short novels to be filled with
       overtones and afterimages which are "inexplicable, un-
       resolved, but oddly affecting." Supports Hawkes's
       "refusal to compromise with the demand for effortless
       intelligibility."

188.   Thurston, Mona.   "Two Novels in One Cover." St.
       Louis Post-Dispatch, August 17, 1954, p. 2C. o
       These novellas display the characteristic dream-
       like quality of Hawkes's other works while, in addi-
       tion, The Owl can be compared to a painting by Hiero-
       nymous Bosch. Both short novels possess the "abso-
       lute sureness of tone, brilliance of detail and use of
       language that enable one to say with certainty ... that
       Mr. Hawkes is an extraordinarily good writer."

189.   "Two Novellas." Nation, July 3, 1954, p. 17. o
       "Determinedly baroque fiction," these short novels
       embody little more than "fascinating stage effects."
       Yet Hawkes's rhythms, which lend the works a dream-
       like and timeless effect, are much like Kafka's. On
       the other hand, Hawkes's images, though "jewel-like,"
       do not blend with the surrounding prose, and his char-
       acters, quite like vivid dream images, lack "suffici-
       ent basis in humanity."

190.   W., L. D. "Goose on the Grave Excellent Short Work."
       Columbia Missourian, July 1, 1954, p. 4. o
       Likens Hawkes's "style of contradiction and para-
       dox" to that of T. S. Eliot and Ezra Pound and con-
       tends that the prose of the novellas is so well done
       "that it can be enjoyed almost without regard to con-
       tent."

191.   Yeiser, Frederick. Review of The Goose on the
       Grave. Cincinnati Enquirer, May 23, 1954, p.
       35. -
       Initially complains about the plethora of images
       and symbols found in the two novels and feels that,

generally, both works will present difficulties to the
reader. Yet, observes that Hawkes is an original
writer, whose prose is "tensely-pitched, highly-
wrought, and poetic."

SEE ALSO: Nos. 223, 250, 317, 449-472.

The Lime Twig

192. Adams, Phoebe. "Potpourri." Atlantic Monthly, No-
      vember 1961, p. 192.
      "Behind its brilliantly evasive style a story worthy
      of Ian Fleming."

193. "Books We Have Enjoyed." John O'London's 7 (Sep-
      tember 27, 1962): 300.
      Written in a style "that is designed to shock and
      to educate," this novel, by "one of the foremost of
      American writers of fiction," bizarrely combines
      Gothic horror with "modern thinking and the author's
      own vision of the human condition."

194. Bradbury, Malcolm. "New Novels." Punch, Oc-
      tober 31, 1962, pp. 647-8. [648] o
      Bradbury holds this to be a "most exceptional
      book" and "anti-novel," a parody of Graham Greene's
      Brighton Rock, and a work which can be properly val-
      ued only by accepting its "highly complex psychologi-
      cal imagery."

195. Cassill, R. V. "Terror in the Grand Sense." New
      Leader, October 30, 1961, pp. 27-8. +
      Proclaims Hawkes's uniqueness, praising his
      "control of style and organization, as well as of pri-
      mary vision." Finds the greatest merit of the book
      to be its expression of "the polymorphous vulnerabil-
      ity of the person as a child would experience it."

196. Daniel, John. "Various Hells." Spectator (London),
      September 21, 1962, p. 410. o
      "Part-parody of a novel, part-parody of reality,"
      this work is, at points, melodramatic and quite over-
      done but forces us to "read with the same concentra-
      tion given to poetry."

197. Dawkins, Cecil. "Horse on a Strange Track: John

Hawkes' Lime Twig." Milwaukee Journal, July
30, 1961, part 5, p. 4. -
The reviewer explains that Hawkes has so few
readers because he destroys the reader's established
concept of reality and then compels him to accept a
reality which is unfamiliar and terrifying. He judges
that the novelist sometimes errs in using too much detail but that, nonetheless, he "recovers to pull off
some remarkable feats."

198.   Didion, Joan. "Notes from a Helpless Reader." Na-
       tional Review, July 15, 1961, pp. 21-2. [22] -
       Confesses inability to convey Hawkes's "imagina-
tive brilliance" but says that the novel's power lies in
its proximity to nightmare, in the fact that it displays
"every waking wish carried to its logical extreme."

199.   Dupee, F. W. "An Imaginary Island." Reporter, July
       20, 1961, pp. 56-7. +
       In treating Michel Butor's Passing Time, as well
as Hawkes's novel, characterizes both authors as in-
tently anti-realistic and Hawkes's work, unlike Butor's,
as "more like Sartre's conception of Faulkner: experience unvitiated by philosophy." Believes that
Hawkes's exceptional powers of invention and prose
style have revived the art of novel-writing.

200.   Guerard, Albert J. "John Hawkes' Geography of Ter-
       ror." New York Herald Tribune, June 25, 1961,
       Lively Arts Section, p. 32. +
       Animatedly, Guerard points out that this novel, by
an undeservedly little-known writer, is an extraordinary "anatomy of terror," whose style is rich and
"exceptionally controlled" and evidences a new interest on Hawkes's part in "story, character, and suspense." He also praises the "rich prose rhythms" and
"intense use of disturbing erotic imagery" in the novel.

201.   Hall, James B. "Hijacking Race Horse Basis for Sur-
       realism." Los Angeles Times, May 7, 1961,
       part C, p. 7. -
       Suggesting by its title to be a metaphor about the
human condition, this highly compressed and precisely
controlled tale of terror depends greatly on Hawkes's
"control of tone, exploitation of language for poetic
effect and ... unerring artistic judgment."

202. Harvey, Elizabeth. "New Fiction." Birmingham
      (England) Post, July 13, 1968, p. 8. o
      In order to read this "veiled, ambiguous writer"
      one must be adventurous and be prepared to delve in-
      to the "mysteries of unreason." While the present
      novel is nightmarish, and one cannot easily identify
      with the characters, Hawkes's pioneering efforts to
      destroy the boundaries of novel-writing should be ad-
      mired.

203. "Into the Atmosphere." Times Literary Supplement,
      August 29, 1968, p. 929. +
      This Gothic romance contains images instead of
      events, a sometimes powerful atmosphere, and rhe-
      torical control that falters at some points. As a
      whole, it is an uneven work that is "often self-indul-
      gent in the exercise of its rhetoric" but is, undeni-
      ably impressive.

204. Lunsford, John. "Style Blunts Tale's Impact." Dal-
      las Morning News, January 21, 1962, sec. 5, p.
      8. o
      The novel's "hectic style and elliptic sequence of
      action" well portray our present incomplete and deper-
      sonalized life and make for intellectual, not emotion-
      al, involvement with the characters. Its effectiveness
      will depend largely on the reader's mood while read-
      ing.

205. McHugh, Vincent. "Authors Wrote Books They Want."
      San Francisco Sunday Chronicle, March 11, 1962,
      This World section, p. 35. o
      Hawkes is a major writer, whether we realize it
      or not. His manner of working with a basic melodra-
      ma of gangsters and an English horse race "almost de-
      fines the difference between storytelling and literature."

206. Mack, Lorna C. "Nightmare Novels." Houston Post,
      April 30, 1961, Houston Now section, p. 37. o
      The terror of this novel, promoted by a mixture
      of "distinct detail and blurred context," is more real
      than that which our everyday entertainment portrays.
      Filled with elaborate descriptions that almost make it
      overwritten, this work is for the reader seeking an
      "intellectual work-out."

207. Mitchell, Julian. "The New 'Brave New World'."

Sunday Times (London), September 30, 1962, p.
32. o
Notes the powerful images and poetically-ex-
pressed episodes, but also the "remoteness" of this
novel. Concludes that "anyone given to a few quiet
minutes of hallucination after meals will like The
Lime Twig. "

208.   Monteiro, George. "A Curve for Violence. " Brown
Review 1 (Summer 1961): 24-6, 28. #
Scholarly, critical remarks, asserting that Hawkes
tries to "reclaim a 'real' realism" by "forcing upon
us a sense of the human reality" within violent acts.
States that the novel depends structurally upon the
"transmutation of imagery and the motif of the private
dream translated into the public act, " as well as upon
the role changes of the characters. Gives extended
explanations of some of the images found in the novel.

209.   Moran, Charles. Review of The Lime Twig. Brown
Herald Supplement 4 (March 28, 1961); 11. +
Precise detail, economically used, makes this novel terrifying, yet credible. Detail, the medium for
portraying abnormal character, is also used "as symbol, echo, reflector. " Hawkes's world-view, that
"forces of disorder" dominate society and the individual, here finds a vivid, terrifying formulation.

210.   O'Donnell, Eugene. Review of The Lime Twig.
Brown Alumni Monthly 61 (May 1961): 25. -
That man cannot prevail against the forces of evil
is the chillingly clear message of Hawkes's powerful,
disturbing, and "technically brilliant" novel. However,
that Hawkes should wallow around in the well-known
fact that "horror is real" is a perverse misuse of a
first-rate talent.

211.   Oliver, Mark. "American in Trouble. " Eastern
Daily Press (Norwich, England), July 19, 1968,
p. 15. o
Values highly Hawkes's abilities in evoking emotions, telling stories and describing situations, and
thinks that the novelist is particularly unusual and for-
tunate enough to have freed himself from the "left-
bank ballyhoo" surrounding some contemporary American writers.

212.   "People Are Talking about ... New Excitements."
            Vogue, July 1961, pp. 36-9. [39]
            The whole statement about Hawkes reads: "Peo-
        ple are talking about ... the indistinct but clearly
        Gothic horror of The Lime Twig by John Hawkes, who
        makes this novel about a race-track fix seem at once
        remarkable, brilliant, and above all uneasy."

213.   Pine, John C. Review of The Lime Twig. Library
            Journal 86 (May 1, 1961): 1794. -
            "A 20th-century journey through the infernal re-
        gions," which is brimful of surprises and delight and
        has resulted from the novelist's skillful mixture of
        "sprightly dialogue" and "dark, moody, introspective"
        prose.

214.   Powers, Dennis. "Journey into Horror in Surrealist
            Thriller." Oakland Tribune, December 14, 1961,
            p. 25. +
            Hails this as a "surrealistic suspense novel--dis-
        jointed ... often outrageous, always eerie, and alto-
        gether fascinating," as well as pervaded by a sense
        of horror. Indicates his gradual discovery of Hawkes's
        artistry and dubs the writer a "brilliant and complete-
        ly unique teller" of tales.

215.   "Quick Looks ... at Fiction." Evening Standard (Lon-
            don), July 30, 1968, p. 8.
            This is a novel, written by "a latter-day Saroy-
        an," which "has become a minor cult in highbrow
        America."

216.   Review of The Lime Twig. New Yorker, April 29,
            1961, p. 149. o
            The novel's "bright flashes of emotion and imag-
        ery" should be better balanced "to provide it [the
        story] with the proportion and perspective that it very
        badly needs." Generally, too, the prose is murky.

217.   Review of The Lime Twig. Times Literary Supple-
            ment, September 21, 1962, p. 746.
            "Told with the inconsequence of a nightmare" and
        possessing some "fashionable sour" touches, the novel
        "concerns an English racing gang and the unpleasant
        things ... which happen to various comparatively inno-
        cent people."

218.   Review of The Lime Twig. Virginia Quarterly Re-
             view 37 (Summer 1961): lxxxii. o
        Hawkes here shows "his insidious, spectacular
        talent for invoking the sinister, accompanied by an
        overwhelming sense of angst."

219.   Richardson, Maurice. "Upper Crusts." New States-
             man, September 21, 1962, pp. 370-1. [370] o
        "A specimen of American tough phoney avant-
        garde writing of a kind that seems to be on the in-
        crease," whose characters "remind you of stock prop-
        erties from the electric typewriter of any old fiction
        factory."

220.   Rosenfield, Claire. "John Hawkes: Nightmares of
             the Real." Minnesota Review 2 (Winter 1962):
             249-54. #
        Suggests that Hawkes's consistent use of nightmar-
        ish distortion makes the reader uncomfortable, even
        though the reader "may never consciously realize that
        he carries these worlds and their obsessive fantasies
        within himself." Presents clear evidence, especially
        in reference to The Lime Twig, of how Hawkes con-
        trols his creative energy so perfectly and how he re-
        veals his technique of terror. Maintains that The
        Lime Twig has "more narrative complexity and less
        surface difficulty" than any earlier novel and displays
        a "more subtle control of symbolism."

221.   Scannell, Vernon. "Distortions." New Statesman,
             July 12, 1968, p. 56. o
        "A highbrow thriller," which presents the violence
        of the underworld in "concentrated images and vivid
        episodes." Yet the book fails because it never forces
        the reader to confront the violence within himself or
        within the world and merely reminds him of other nov-
        els.

222.   Schott, Webster. "Some Books of '61 Join Notable
             Reading from Past." Kansas City Times, Janu-
             ary 16, 1962, p. 24. o
        Confidently stating that Hawkes "has already cre-
        ated the most impressive body of American distortion-
        al literature" of which he is cognizant, Schott admires
        Hawkes's insistence on presenting his conception of the
        human condition within his works, despite the reader's

emotional rejection of this valid view.   He interprets
The Lime Twig on one level in accordance with
Hawkes's view, saying that it shows "the destruction
of love through the debasement of most of what is hu-
mane in human kind. "

223. _____. "Vision of a Nightmare." Nation, September 2, 1961, pp. 122-3; excerpted in Modern
American Literature, p. 51. (No. 587). #
Hawkes is "an American original," whose novels
are "both visionary and circumvolved, expressing a
highly individualistic conception of the dread, terror
and calamity that confront humankind. " His Charivari
is very conceivably a "tragicomedy about wickedness
of caste and the collapse of sex," while The Cannibal
concerns itself with impotent sex, a decomposing
world, and "the universal triumph of evil," The Beetle
Leg parodies the "Western," and The Owl and The
Goose on the Grave, filled with anticlericalism and
antiauthoritarianism, both lament "the failure of action and an epidemic human resignation to defect and
consequent destruction. " All of these novels, as well
as The Lime Twig, also share similarities in technique and theme.   However, The Lime Twig, whose
"recitations of inhumanity" ring true to life, shows
evidence of Hawkes's new control over his imagination
and prose style.
Influences on Hawkes's writing range from T. S.
Eliot to Freud, but, unfortunately, few are willing to
study his forceful, imaginary works.   Many have yet
to be convinced that this fiction is comparable to contemporary European fiction and drama of the same
motivation.

224. Seymour-Smith, Martin. "Sex and the Woman, by
Edna O'Brien." Oxford (England) Mail, July 4,
1968, p. 10. o
John Hawkes, "a leading American novelist" who
has received far less attention than he deserves, produces exceedingly difficult, but highly original and rewarding works.   In particular, The Lime Twig is
"one of the few novels of the Sixties that deserves to
be read through twice. "

225. Todd, Richard S. "The Lime Twig." Amherst Student, May 1, 1961, p. 2. +
Critics rightly praise Hawkes's ability to create

nightmares; for, this talented novelist's latest work "exudes fear" as it maintains a "general atmosphere of disorder" and provides horrible details in neat, powerful sentences. Fiedler's rationale for the work (see No. 530), concentrating on the book's formlessness, can easily be rejected, but not so easily this unusual, effective fiction.

226.   Troy, George. "Remarque's Latest and a Gothic
           Horror." Providence Sunday Journal, April 9,
           1961, p. W-20. -
        The Lime Twig is a "genuine Gothic horror story," whose mood is "permeated with an extraordinarily bitter sadism." Its stylistic precision and economy is easily appreciated, but its nightmarish mood and effects will not be tolerated by many readers for long.

227.   Weisberg, Edzia. "Fiction Chronicle." Partisan Re-
           view 28, No. 5-6 (1961): 716-22. [716-7] -
        This novelist's gift for language is seen in the novel's powerful imagery and syntax and "vivid local evocations."   However, Hawkes's one great disadvantage--his commitment to anti-realism--has brought him to the point of creating merely spectacles "of the irrational and horrifying." He ought to overcome his self-indulgence and eliminate the "weird" elements from his works.

228.   West, Ray B. "After the Blitz." New York Times
           Book Review, May 14, 1961, p. 31; excerpted in
           Modern American Literature, p. 51 (No. 587). -
        West asserts that Hawkes's latest work of fiction, in which the events are "skillfully and meaningfully portrayed," is quite readable, "moves the reader to a genuine pathos, and sheds a glow of understanding on our times." He thinks that the writer is attempting to provide an answer in this book to the question: "What are the possibilities of, and terms for, the creation of the hero in our time?"

SEE ALSO: Nos. 164, 235, 248, 250, 274, 308, 334.

Second Skin

229.   Adams, Robert M. "Hit and Miss." New York Re-
           view of Books, April 2, 1964, pp. 12-3. *

Deems <u>Second Skin</u> to be a "work of gifted maturity," in which the story is really a "sequence of
explanations" and the style is "not tricksy, not calis-
thenic, but consciously alive and vibrant as one of
Papa Cue Ball's favorite humming birds." With an
artistic flair and much obvious enjoyment introduces
both the characters and "story."

230.   Alderman, Nancy. <u>Review of Second Skin.</u> Nash-
       <u>ville Tennessean,</u> March 29, 1964, p. 6-D. +
       Hawkes's tragi-comic novel offers an interpreta-
       tion of the much-discussed concept of "survivorship,"
       since it presents a character (Skipper), who personi-
       fies "Man controlled by Fate" and who survives physi-
       cally, morally, and emotionally. The work is intend-
       ed to irritate, as well as challenge, the reader to the
       point of goading him to re-evaluate his life.

231.   Allsop, Kenneth. "Cockroaches and Kools." <u>Specta-</u>
       <u>tor</u> (London), January 28, 1966, pp. 113-4.
       Describes the novelist's style as "coy and veiled,"
       in which "the bitter-sweet of James Purdy is thickened
       to a curd with Nabokovian archness."

232.   Bell, Vereen. "Son of Billy Budd Meets Naked
       Lunch." <u>Shenandoah</u> 16 (Winter 1965): 63-6. *
       Praises Hawkes's impressionistic and surrealistic
       technique, seeing symbolism, allegory, and poetry in
       the novelist's works. With respect to <u>Second Skin,</u>
       gives a lengthy explanation of Skipper's personality and
       indicates how the other characters in the novel affect
       Skipper. Ultimately, feels that like Defoe's <u>Moll</u>
       <u>Flanders</u> this book was intended to show the "abrasive
       texture of existence," but is really a comedy of the
       same ilk as <u>Don Quixote.</u>

233.   Berridge, Elizabeth. "Self before Family." <u>Daily</u>
       <u>Telegraph</u> (London), January 27, 1966, p. 21. o
       A story about a highly-resilient narrator, Skipper,
       written in mesmeric language and including several
       haunting scenes.

234.   Breid, Jan. "All the Coherence of a 'Nightmare'."
       <u>Columbia Missourian,</u> May 3, 1964, p. 11. o
       Here is a "disturbing book" with unforgettable de-
       scriptions and an intangible dream-like quality.
       Hawkes has created "beauty even in the sordid" but

makes us question how individual incidents combine to
arrive at a deeper meaning for the novel.

235.   Brooks, Peter. "John Hawkes." Encounter (London),
         June 1966, pp. 68-72; reprinted in The Merrill
         Studies in Second Skin, pp. 13-8 (No. 537); ex-
         cerpted and translated into French as the "Pref-
         ace." In Cassandra, by John Hawkes, pp. 11-8.
         Paris: Denoël, 1968 (No. 6d).
         Works of fiction by John Hawkes have always
         been "uncompromisingly difficult and often extraordi-
         narily beautiful." The Cannibal, "an historico-apoca-
         lyptic surrealistic vision of a brutalized race," lacks
         "an identifiable narrative tone" or "overall narrative
         coherence." On the other hand, in The Lime Twig,
         through manipulation of the conventions of a thriller,
         Hawkes succeeds in giving us a "sense of overwhelm-
         ing lucidity about our relations to others, and to our-
         selves, a monstrous clarity about our passions." Fi-
         nally, Second Skin benefits from the novelist's re-
         markable control of language and application of senses
         and an imagination that are totally alive and appears
         as a work of Hawkes's "mature clarity," "a clarity
         of the senses, a clarity of emotional landscapes ren-
         dered in full sensuous dimension."

236.   Burgess, Anthony. "New Fiction." Listener, Febru-
         ary 3, 1966, p. 181.
         Burgess admires the novel's "genuine texture,"
         in which "disparate colours are woven into a pattern
         that is seen, after the shocks, to be inevitable." He
         believes, then, that Hawkes's is the only possible way
         to tell Skipper's story.

237.   Carruth, Hayden. "New Hawkes Novel Rich in Spirit
         and Style." Chicago Daily News, March 28, 1964,
         p. 7. *
         The reviewer proclaims that this is a "real book,"
         a simple story which is pervaded by the atmosphere
         of war and ends in "one of the liveliest pastorales of
         all prose fiction." He feels that Hawkes, whose most
         important virtue is his independence from any "mere-
         ly fashionable influence," has continued to strengthen
         his style and intellectual progress towards understand-
         ing of human reality, and is "our best young novel-
         ist."

238. Darack, Arthur. "It Pays to Quiver This Way Pub-
       licly." Cincinnati Enquirer, April 11, 1964, p.
       40. +
       Hawkes's skill with language is his greatest asset,
       and this novel is "superb, full of ingenious and poetic
       combination [sic] of word and deed, and some first-
       rate plotting and characterization." Since Hawkes is
       not a moralist, he presents a narrator with neither
       any faults nor any virtues, who is actually "insuffi-
       ciently a child of fate." Skipper is too much like a
       Greek tragic hero for my tastes.

239. Derleth, August. "An Arresting Novelist." Capital
       Times (Madison, Wisc.), May 8, 1964, p. 8. o
       "One of the most important American novelists
       writing today," John Hawkes, has produced this com-
       ic novel, "a brilliant composite," which draws intelli-
       gent readers with its unique prose style. The work
       is a compelling, though nightmarish, creation.

240. Elrond. "Book Bazaar." Harper's Bazaar, May 1964,
       pp. 29, 59. [59] o
       Appreciates Hawkes's "rich, dense" style but dis-
       likes his use of "droning inventories of detail," repe-
       tition of certain phrases, and frequent unintelligibility,
       as seen in this work. Recommends the novel, though,
       because of its plot, imaginative power, and eloquent
       descriptions.

241. F., P. C. "Experiments Are Interesting Failures."
       Sacramento Bee, July 5, 1964, p. L-17. o
       For the reader interested in modern fiction this
       novel, full of biting wit and comic elements, is a val-
       uable addition to the body of literary works attempting
       to solve the problem of how to write about contempo-
       rary life. The weakness of this "story of survival,"
       however, lies in its overemphasis on technique.

242. Fauchereau, Serge. "Un Romancier américain inso-
       lite." La Quinzaine littéraire (Paris), May 1-15,
       1968, p. 6. +
       Calls Hawkes the most unusual and most unap-
       preciated contemporary American novelist and a prop-
       er successor to Faulkner. Admires Hawkes's style,
       especially his lyricism, and believes that the novelist's
       main interest in writing is to portray the human condi-
       tion. Although noting the clear narrative in Second Skin,

warns the reader that this novel arouses conflicting
emotions concerning whether or not to sympathize
with the characters.

243.   Fink, Michael. "Son of Death Seeks Life." Provi-
        dence Sunday Journal, April 19, 1964, p. W-20.
        +
        Though weary of the novel's depressing episodes
        and listings of bad odors, reveals the nature of Skip-
        per's temperament and gives an outline of this "elab-
        orate allegory." Concludes with the prediction that
        "those who enjoy a weird picture puzzle will revel in
        it."

244.   Galloway, David. "A Dichotomy of Islands." Trace,
        No. 53 (1964), pp. 181-4. *
        Over the years Hawkes's experimental stance has
        been modified and the physical landscapes of his nov-
        els have changed radically, but his use of a psychic
        landscape in which "barrenness and brutality of a mass
        mind as it slides ominously toward self-destruction or
        gross inconsequence" is exposed remains constant.
        Hawkes's idiosyncratic style, employing highly visual
        prose and consistent juxtaposition of terror and love,
        death and birth, is more nightmarish than that of Na-
        thanael West and in this work serves a more humani-
        tarian and optimistic purpose than previously; for, it
        has produced Skipper's apologia pro vita sua.

245.   Halio, Jay L. "Second Skins." Southern Review n. s.
        4 (Winter 1968): 236-47. [236-8] +
        Treating the theme of regeneration, this novel
        employs comic development. It is like The Tempest
        in its use of imagery and setting, and Cymbeline with
        respect to its brutal and horrible scenes. Unlike
        these works, however, it fails to separate distinctly
        the "evil past" from the "hopeful present," since
        flashbacks juxtapose past and present events at every
        turn. Christian, or more specifically Catholic, sym-
        bolism and myth abound in the novel, but the result is
        a paean to a "natural Christian religion."

246.   Hanzo, T. A. "The Two Faces of Matt Donelson."
        Sewanee Review 73 (Winter 1965): 106-19. [111-
        4] *
        Second Skin presents a new kind of hero in Skip-
        per--an anti-hero who survives "in defiance, in indig-

nation, and in the sheer perversity of the will to
live." Indeed, Skipper appears to restore a primitive
heroism, and Hawkes's stylistic effects have been motivated by the desire to articulate this type of heroism. Moreover, Hawkes's unusual stylistic devices
were partially chosen "to create the emotional life" in
new, but never sensational or perverse, ways.

247.   Hicks, Granville. "Lover in the Strangeness of Life."
       Saturday Review, March 28, 1964, 25-6. *
       A reading of merely the first paragraph of this
novel proves Hawkes's writing ability. Gradually, the
obscurity of these beginning lines yields to an understanding of the various stylistic devices--the disregard
of chronological ordering to gain emotional impact, the
emphasis on trivial details to contribute to the dreamlike, if not hallucinatory, atmosphere, and others.
This "novel about survival" also offers more extraordinary scenes than Hawkes's other fictions, although,
like the previous novels, it expresses the novelist's
"almost unbearable awareness of the strangeness of
life."

248.   Holmes, Nancy. "Experiments with Purple Prose."
       FOCUS/ Midwest 3 (June 1964): 26-7. +
       With mixed reactions reports that Hawkes's experi-
mentation continues and that, as in his earlier works,
the author "operates against the grain of reality as we
prefer to view it." Finds that this book treats the
same theme as The Lime Twig but that it contains
more "purple prose" and comic overtones "where absurdity stands for ridiculousness (or even hilarity) as
well as tragedy."

249.   Hone, Ralph E. "A 20th-century Tempest." Los Ange-
       les Times, September 27, 1964, Calendar section,
       p. 1. o
       Here is a modern adaptation of The Tempest,
amazingly varied in its tempo, mood, and texture and
written in a style which "suggests that by indirections
we may find directions out."

250.   Hyman, Stanley Edgar. "The Abomination of Desola-
       tion." New Leader, March 30, 1964, pp. 24-5.
       *
       Hyman declares that he finds Hawkes's novels un-
enjoyable and unsuccessful. Nevertheless, in view of

the novelist's "unique role and utter integrity" he analyzes each of them. The Cannibal he calls "the most
depressing and compelling" of Hawkes's works; The
Beetle Leg, "the most Faulknerian ... in the bad
sense of the word"; The Owl, "a dark fable of pointless sacrifice and divine indifference" and Hawkes's
most Kafkaesque fiction; The Goose on the Grave, a
novel of covert homosexuality and "beautiful anticleri-
cal simplicity"; and Second Skin, the only one of the
books to end happily. Despite admitting the existence
of some remarkable scenes in these novels, he disap-
proves of their formlessness and designates them as
"shredded fables, jumbles of apocalyptic visions,"
needing recomposing to turn them into real novels.

251.   Isaacs, Neil D. "Late Getter-In-Onner Digs Hawkes
        Early." Nashville Tennessean, August 16, 1964,
        p. 10-F. +
        "A brilliant novel," whose title has several pos-
        sible meanings and whose action is on two levels, one
        conveying the "therapeutic purgation of Skipper's past"
        and the other, the reconstruction of Skipper's past. It
        treats the violence of our day in an "honest and gentle,
        humanistic and humane" manner.

252.   Isbell, John. "Complexity of Style Overshadows
        Story." Birmington (Ala.) News, April 19, 1964,
        p. E-7.
        Flippantly indicates the uniqueness and complexity
        of Hawkes's style in Second Skin and says, with a cer-
        tain disgust, that Hawkes's method will be studied by
        numerous creative writing students.

253.   Jackson, Katherine Gauss. "Books in Brief." Harp-
        er's Magazine, June 1964, pp. 120-3. [122] +
        An unusual, highly symbolic novel of "furious in-
        tensity." "Scenes of passion, horror, violence usual-
        ly happen against backgrounds so minutely observed
        that the inner eye is enlarged almost beyond endurance
        by the tension between the action and the details around
        it."

254.   Kattan, Naim. "Voyage au bout du cauchemar."
        Critique (Paris) 27 (July 1971): 666-8. +
        Demonstrates that the novel centers around Skip-
        per, who is trying to forge a path between two reali-
        ties--an inner and an outer--although Skipper's con-

cept of reality is that which he creates or invents.
Feels, also, that the book teaches the reader how to
acquire wisdom by submitting himself to life's brutali-
ties and then surmounting them. Concludes, finally,
with the statement that, though like Bellow, Barth,
and other modern American novelists Hawkes writes
literature of anger and despair in new and different
ways, he does so in a poetic manner.

255.   Katz, Bill.   Review of Second Skin.   Library Journal
            89 (April 1, 1964): 1622. o
      "Highly recommended," this work of a major
American novelist recalls the writings of the French
New Realists. Here, Skipper, a "20th-century Can-
dide, Hamlet, existentialist unaware, or what the
reader will, suggests the answer to horror and tragedy
is resignation buttressed by faith in self and life."

256.   Kauffmann, Stanley.   "Further Adventures of the Nov-
            el."   New Republic, June 6, 1964, pp. 19-20,
            22; reprinted in The Merrill Studies in Second
            Skin, pp. 5-8 (No. 537); excerpted in Modern
            American Literature, pp. 51-2 (No. 587).   *
      A novelist "whose reputation is small but smolder-
ing under the haystack of potential large acclaim,"
Hawkes writes novels that are called surrealistic but
are created according to his own definition of the novel form. In his present work there are a few touches
of The Tempest and a structure that can be likened to
that of a "19th Century opera libretto." Its prose is
gorgeous and remarkably imagistic, but its topography
is flattened by the very intense, poetic manner in
which everything is treated. Hawkes is disappointing,
then, because he subordinates the subject matter to
the rendering so that, for the most part, the medium
becomes the object.

257.   King, Francis.   "All the Dregs."   Sunday Telegraph
            (London), January 30, 1966, p. 24.
      Maintains that the novel, despite its beauteous,
poetic style is self-indulgent and "suffers from an imaginative debility."

258.   Lemon, Lee T.   "Art of a Novel."   Prairie Schooner
            39 (Spring 1965): 83.   -
      Though showing the influences of Faulkner, Joyce,
and Bellow, this is a "highly original novel." Some

could praise it for its technique; others, for its demonstration of how a man conquers his "private hells."
It is, above all, "good to read."

259.   Levine, George. "A Courageous Nightmare." Louis-
        ville Courier-Journal, April 5, 1964, sec. 4, p.
        5. +
        While praising Hawkes's rich, imaginative prose
and the book's "extraordinary mixture of the natural-
istic and the fantastic," the reviewer criticizes the
brilliant style for coming between the reader and the
experience to the point that the style becomes the experience. He also calls the work a "long, courageous nightmare of American life" and Skipper, a "Don
Quixote with ideal unarticulated."

260.   Levine, Paul. "Individualism and the Traditional
        Talent." Hudson Review 17 (Autumn 1964): 470-
        7. [475-6]; excerpted in Modern American Litera-
        ture, pp. 52-3 (No. 587). o
        Thinks that "Second Skin's snake's-eye view of a
spiritual underworld is often verbally exciting and visu-
ally rewarding" and admires Hawkes's originality.
However, in closing, remarks that Hawkes's "toler-
ance for bizarre effects remains a defect of his imagination."

261.   McHugh, Vincent. "Hawkes' Latest Is a Classic Com-
        edy." San Francisco Sunday Chronicle, March 14,
        1965, This World section, p. 24. -
        "A rich and endearing book" by an impressive
writer, who has managed to "pin down the vivid sense
of an experience" and has depicted the "inhumanity of
our time." Unfortunately, the lack of a plot in the
normal sense is detrimental to the work.

262.   McMurtry, Larry. "Two Exoticists." Houston Post,
        April 5, 1964, p. 21. o
        Recommendations for Hawkes's works abound, but,
in my estimation, Second Skin has never been enjoyable. Some of its scenes are vivid and arresting,
"but these quickly sink out of sight in a swamp of bad
prose."

263.   Madden, David. "Enemies of Love." Kenyon Review
        26 (Summer 1964): 576-81. [576-9]
        The appeal, impact, and meaning of this novel

come from its images, which embody the forces of
life and death. Although its style is overdone, allowing us merely to bask in the warmth of its rhetoric
and not to penetrate to the underlying experience, the
book is "a rare experience."

264.   Malin, Irving. "Jerky Voyage." Progressive, May
            1964, pp. 48-9.   -
        Says that Hawkes forces the reader, as well as
Skipper, to face such questions as: "Do we ever get
out of ourselves? Can we love each other?" Notes
that Skipper succeeds in his struggles because he lets
life live him. Adds, too, that the repeated images
supply order to the novel and that the "stylistic tension between chaos and order" provides the " 'positive'
meaning of Skipper's existence."

265.   Olson, Ivan. "Able Young Novelist Pens Rich, Night-
            marish Creation." Fresno Bee, April 5, 1964,
            Country Life section, p. 23-F.   -
        "One of our ablest novelists," Hawkes has, none-
theless, produced fictions which are "a little too rich
for the blood this side of the Atlantic." His Second
Skin, along with his earlier novels, deserves a wider
audience; for, in all of his works he uses avant-garde
devices with originality and power, and in this latest
book he portrays Skipper as Everyman.

266.   Parriot, Michael and Snyder, Carl. Review of Second
            Skin. Brown Daily Herald Review 2 (April 1964):
            26-8.   *
        Discover in this work humane ideals, which "pro-
vide the necessary cohesive to endow an apparently
fragmented reality with a universal significance." Con-
tend that Hawkes is a realist who is seeking the reader's psychological identification with the characters,
but that since such an identification reveals repugnant
motivations, the reader will not acknowledge them as
his own. Yet, see this disturbing novel as a story of
love--a love which is the salvation of mankind.

267.   Ratcliffe, Michael. "Liberation in Belfast." Sunday
            Times (London): January 30, 1966, p. 47.   -
        "A series of almost hallucinatory recollections that
advances with increasing facility but rarely puts down
any real roots." While the images over-decorate the
work, the use of recurrent obsessions, attention-hold-

in scenes, and set pieces make the novel work.

268.   Review of Second Skin.   Kirkus 31 (December 1,
             1963): 1119. o
        Notes the light tone and skillful style of the novel
        but foresees that the "misty situations" and "mon-
        strous human furies attacking Skipper's visceral vac-
        uum will not endear Skipper to the American multi-
        tudes."

269.   Ricks, Christopher. "Chamber of Horrors." New
             Statesman, March 11, 1966, pp. 339-40; reprinted
             in The Merrill Studies in Second Skin, pp. 9-12
             (No. 537). *
        Hawkes's novel is far from being a work of sen-
        sationalism or a "chamber of horrors." It is saved
        from such charges by its humor, poetical rhythms,
        and use of classical mythology.   Certainly, the latter
        is the greatest reason for Hawkes's success since he
        chose this apt method of depicting the world's terror
        rather than reverting to English superstition, as the
        English Gothic novelists did, and thus avoided the
        "hectic rhetoric of terror" which appeared in the work
        of those novelists.   Second Skin's fragmentariness is
        but a minor flaw in comparison with all that is ad-
        mirable about it.

270.   Rovit, Earl H.   "Novel Shows Seamy Side of Exist-
             ence."   Richmond News Leader, June 17, 1964,
             p. 7. +
        Undeniably, Hawkes is "one of the incomparable
        prose stylists in contemporary letters," and his latest
        novel is "an exquisitely wrought pendant, garish and
        delicate." Second Skin is, further, the most recent
        example of how Hawkes presents "the seamy banalities
        of life in their grossness" and forces the reader "to
        respond to them as evil," but effects these results
        poetically and sensuously.   The title, by the way, re-
        fers to the "emotion-proof shelter" within which Skip-
        per has been enveloped since his father's death.

271.   Sanders, Nicholas.   "Dark Comedy Prevails in Man's
             Second Chance." Nashville Banner, April 10,
             1964, p. 27. -
        Lying somewhere between "the pseudo-artistic
        writers ... and the mainstream of the avant-garde,"
        Hawkes writes "peculiarly believable and slightly

wacky novels," which are appropriately termed black
comedy and which "take place in the too-strongly
lighted livingroom of mankind's unwillingly awakened
conscience." In the present novel Hawkes's success
is that he has made Skipper "a true hero, a believ-
able and acceptable person."

272.   Schott, Webster. "The World of John Hawkes is
       Brutal, But Loving Also." Kansas City Star, Ap-
       ril 26, 1964, p. 6-G. +
       Without hesitation one should call this work a su-
       perior novel by one of the "finest original writers
       working in the United States." It "sees the world
       true--impersonally cruel, comically sinister, and
       abundant with possibilities for love." Interlaced with
       terror and comedy, two themes appear: the conten-
       tion that "survival is a complex and brutal business"
       and the "sacrificial nature of love in all its varie-
       ties," including unconscious incestuous leanings. Ful-
       filling a moral purpose, this novel displays man defi-
       antly surviving all of his experiences.

273.   Seward, William W. "Skin of Despair Shed." Virgin-
       ian-Pilot, May 3, 1964, p. B-6. -
       Considers the virtue of this impressive novel, "the
       story of a man's survival in a destructive world," to
       lie in its indescribable style.

274.   "Skin Deep." Times Literary Supplement, February
       17, 1966, p. 117. -
       Agrees that Hawkes is an experimental writer but
       objects to the present novel's unconvincing background
       and mixed-up chronology. Also bemoans Hawkes's
       penchant for "unnecessary occlusions," his "inability
       to spot and control unintentionally farcical elements,"
       and his lapses into "apostrophizing rhetoric."

275.   Sontag, Susan. "A New Life for an Old One." New
       York Times Book Review, April 5, 1964, p. 5;
       reprinted in The Merrill Studies in Second Skin,
       pp. 3-5 (No. 537). *
       Ms. Sontag's often-quoted estimation of Hawkes as
       "one of the half dozen authors of first rank in Ameri-
       ca today" appears here. Referring to the present nov-
       el, she calls it Skipper's apologia pro vita sua, whose
       theme is "horror surmounted by lushness and love."
       Barely mentioning the faults she finds with Hawkes's

works, she emphasizes instead her admiration for the
novelist's exact observation, "beautifully realized ...
'scenes'," wonderfully visual writing, and, especially,
his "looped, virile, restless style that really is the
story."

276.   Stafford, Jean. "Ricocheting with Papa Cue Ball."
       New York Herald Tribune, April 19, 1964, Book
       Week, pp. 5, 15. *
       As we can see from numerous examples taken
       from this novel, Hawkes is oblivious to chronology and
       straightforward character delineation. But the novel-
       ist has produced a work which, because of Skipper's
       amour propre, is both "satisfying and serious."
       Stylistically, Hawkes appears to have written part of
       the novel in incompleted dithyrambs and another "in
       a highly idiomatic Hawkesian vernacular, wry, ribald,
       terrifying, cool."

277.   Steele, William O. "Making Peace with Reality."
       Chattanooga Times, June 21, 1964, p. 16.
       "A serpentine novel about an anti-hero" who man-
       ages to "survive his losing bouts with reality."

278.   Thompson, Francis J. "Four Views of Women--and
       Their Role." Roanoke Times, May 17, 1964, p.
       B-12. o
       Views the work as an expression of the opinion
       that "women eternally want to drive man to self-de-
       struction." However, expresses pleasure in reading
       this "example of un-Wordsworthian emotions recalled
       in tranquillity."

279.   Trachtenberg, Stanley. "Counterhumor: Comedy in
       Contemporary American Fiction." Georgia Review
       27 (Spring 1973): 33-48. [40-2] +
       In this novel "the comic affirmation of the artifi-
       cial is echoed in the narrative style as well as devel-
       oped in thematic content." For example, the color
       green, commonly indicating organic renewal of life,
       becomes symbolic of the "perverse submission of life
       to death." Skipper, unable to stem this submission
       and, in part, aiding its continuation, nonetheless re-
       fuses to accept his position as victim in this process
       as definitive and ultimately becomes an artificial in-
       seminator, resulting in a "triumph of the artificial
       over the natural."

280. Tracy, Robert. Review of <u>Second Skin</u>. <u>Ramparts,</u>
      October 1964, pp. 61-2.   *
           Like <u>Moby Dick,</u> another "important failure," <u>Sec-</u>
      <u>ond Skin</u> "leaves us with a degree of frustration and
      dissatisfaction, and yet with a haunting awareness of
      presences that cannot be dismissed." Hawkes has
      here produced a powerful novel, which, in its portray-
      al of a fragmentary world and human discontinuity can
      be likened to the poetry of T. S. Eliot. On the other
      hand, it is overwritten and has its "dark vision" con-
      trolled far too much by a logical and obvious scheme
      based on allusion.

281. Wardle, Irving. "Faust in the Kitchen." <u>Observer</u>
      <u>Weekend Review</u> (London), January 23, <u>1966, p.</u>
      <u>27.</u> o
           Cannot see Hawkes's purpose in eliminating nor-
      mal time elements from the novel and is irritated by
      the novelist's use of "loquacious telegraphese." En-
      joys only the book's "close-up description."

282. Wensberg, Erik. "Books." <u>Vogue,</u> January 1, 1964,
      p. 22; reprinted in The <u>Merrill Studies in Second</u>
      Skin, p. 2 (No. 537). -
           So real, so authentic are the characters in this
      novel that we cannot escape noticing how they prove
      "the evil in life." Oblique allusions to Shakespeare
      and myth also appear throughout the work, attesting
      also to the fact that "we have no more gifted novel-
      ist" than Hawkes.

SEE ALSO: Nos. 334, 339, 368.

The Blood Oranges

283. Baker, Roger. Review of <u>The Blood Oranges</u>. <u>Books</u>
      <u>and Bookmen</u> 17 (December 1971): 64. o
           Reading this novel is "like sinking ever deeper
      into a warm, damp bunch of highly-scented flowers.
      Very sensuous, very lyrical, but with no thorns on
      the roses," although there is a definite need for
      thorns.

284. Bawden, Nina. "Recent Fiction." <u>Daily Telegraph</u>
      (London), November 11, 1971, p. 8.
           "A highly symbolic and very dignified sexual fan-
      tasy," told in "beautifully measured, elliptical prose"

and passages of high comedy. Hawkes could be
called, perhaps, the intellectual's Iris Murdoch.

285.   Beacham, Walton. "Hawkes' New Novel Imparts Nag-
            ging Sense of Importance." Richmond Times-
            Dispatch, December 5, 1971, p. F-5.   +
        Telling of Hawkes's "considerable reputation,"
suspects that because of the language and technique of
this latest book, which is like those of many other
contemporary writers, it may be considered a good
novel in time to come. Yet judges the work to be un-
inspiring and sloppily done, due in part to characters
and some symbols that are not developed enough and
to other symbols that are too blatant.

286.   Bell, Pearl K. "Dull Decay and Exuberant Comedy."
            New Leader, October 4, 1971, pp. 17-8.   *
        Throughout his career Hawkes has steadfastly pur-
sued his portrayal of the "terrifying similarity between
the unconscious desire of the solitary man and the destructive needs of the visible world" by describing un-
speakably horrible incidents in his works. However,
this new novel is lapidary and soporific. It could be
a parody of Lawrence Durrell's " 'poetic' quasi-por-
nography." But, whatever the intent, it is "only a
stereotyped experiment with hyperbole of the senses,
in pinchbeck prose that struts and preens as though it
were authentic coin of the realm."

287.   Bianciotti, Hector. "L'Île inaccessible." Le Nouvel
            observateur (Paris), August 13-19, 1973, p. 51.
            +
        Citing several critics and writers who highly ap-
preciate Hawkes's novels, Bianciotti offers his own
opinion that the novelist's reputation will be enlarged
by this newest work. Outlining the story of the novel,
he points out its sad ending, in which the tapestry of
love becomes torn, despite Cyril's inadmission of the
fact. His final statements concern his feeling that the
theme of the book is much like that told by Ulysses:
A king leaves home to fight in battle and in returning
to his island home encounters many obstacles along
the way. Only in Hawkes's use of the theme, he says,
Ulysses himself becomes the inaccessible island, whose
resident weaver forms a tapestry telling the story of
all of us.

288. Black, Stephen A. "John Hawkes, The Blood Oranges."
        West Coast Review 7 (October 1972): 76-7.   +
        "A little vulgarity might have helped this blood-
      less academic exercise, but nothing could save it."
      Its new terms are "blatantly hypocritical," while Cyr-
      il's lyrical statements are pompous and false. Al-
      though it is supposedly a "comic alternative to total
      cataclysmic collapse ... it is only childish self-justi-
      fication trying to pass for a liberated moral vision."

289. Briggs, Edwin. "An Idyler in Illyria." Boston Sun-
        day Globe, September 12, 1971, p. 18-A.   +
        Discusses the setting and the characters, espe-
      cially Cyril. Finds that Cyril, "the most elaborate-
      ly decorated subject of his own style--weaving," in-
      variably presents his thoughts in fine-sounding, lyri-
      cal phrases but appears to "miss the complex reality
      of all human relationship" in his "polyandrous version
      of pastoral."

290. Bruni, Thomas G. Review of The Blood Oranges.
        Lehigh Valley Labor Herald (Allentown, Pa.),
        September 29, 1971, p. 3.   -
        Persevering readers will discover in this, and in
      all other fictions by Hawkes, evidence of the novel-
      ist's "powerful and penetrating" imagination and "pre-
      cise and steady" prose. The Blood Oranges revolves
      around Cyril, a "dazzling creation" and the figure of
      a "thoroughly modern man caught in the prison he
      fashioned for himself but unaware of it."

291. Byatt, A. S. "The Bitter-sweet Delights of Arcadia."
        Times (London), December 20, 1971, p. 9-g.   -
        Introduces the characters and the "plot" of this
      "work of art, a highly patterned novel exploiting the
      essential ambivalences of our attitude to the bitter-
      sweet delights of Illyria." Cautions that the meaning
      of this brilliant book is complex, though noting the
      readily observable flowing style and "glowing, precise
      sensual, chilling" prose.

292. Cabau, Jacques. "Les Rêves interdits de John
        Hawkes." L'Express, August 13-19, 1973, pp.
        49-50.   +
        Touching first upon The Cannibal, Hawkes's state-
      ment about our "cannibalistic" civilization, talks next
      of the novelist's style, through which is created a

world lying somewhere between waking and sleeping,
distorted by terror, mystery, and parody, and filled
with suspended action and a spellbinding combination
of reality and imagination. Considers the present
novel to be, above all, a comedy in the manner of
Nabokov and evidence that Hawkes's astonishing vision
has reached its maturity.

293.   Carver, Wayne. "Fiction." Esquire, January 1972,
            pp. 33-4, 150. [34, 150] +
        An important novel, whose style is one of its ma-
jor creations but whose theme is essentially Jamesian
--"the perfection of the aesthetic sense at the expense
of the moral one." Indeed, Cyril can be likened to
Chad Newsome of The Ambassadors or, even more
so, to Gilbert Osmond of The Portrait of a Lady.

294.   Collins, Thomas. "Spotlighting a 'Dark' Novelist."
            Newsday (Garden City, N. Y.), October 25, 1971,
            p. 13A. +
        Demonstrates by using passages from The Lime
Twig and The Blood Oranges that Hawkes's poetic style
"reflects his preoccupation with the rhythms and juxta-
positions of language." Maintains, further, that solely from imagination Hawkes has developed "intellectual terror" as one of his trademarks and has no literary ancestor, with the possible exception of Faulkner.
Emphasizes Hawkes's intellectual background, adding
that the novelist himself feels that he is "bothered by
the Puritan ethic."

295.   De Feo, Ronald. Review of The Blood Oranges.
            Saturday Review, October 23, 1971, pp. 92, 94.
            +
        "A unique talent in American fiction," Hawkes
has always produced first-rate nightmares and has
demonstrated "a remarkable ability to create dream
landscapes." Though showing his tendency to over-
write "badly like Lawrence Durrell," in this novel
Hawkes presents clever, fascinating scenes about "the
multiplicity and complexity of 'love'."

296.   Ditsky, John. "The Man on the Quaker Oats Box:
            Characteristics of Recent Experimental Fiction."
            Georgia Review 26 (Fall 1972): 297-313. [301-
            3] +
        Hawkes's works are outstanding examples of the

experimental technique of allowing the story line to be
dominated by "the sheer physical presence of a 'dream'
landscape." While the present novel ostensibly is the
most conventional of all of Hawkes's fictions, its
"finely-textured landscape contrasts with the circular-
ity of his story line" and allows mental state and ex-
terior image to merge beyond all reasonable expecta-
tions. Such a landscape is "a tapestry in which we
recognize our deepest selves."

297.   Dorheim, Jean. "Blood on the Ways." Milwaukee
        Journal, October 10, 1971, part 5, p. 4. o
        Dreamlike and highly visual, The Blood Oranges
intentionally contains characters that are "more like
figures in an heroic frieze than like real people" and
suggests "an intricate and formal tapestry, conceived
of gryphons, unicorns and the insatiable appetites of
the gods."

298.   Fine, Warren. "Books & People: Cyril Sings of
        Sex." Boston Phoenix, December 1, 1971, pp.
        28, 30-1. #
        Charging that no one is literate in the contempo-
rary American novel who has not read Second Skin or
The Lime Twig, proceeds to give a lengthy interpretation of The Blood Oranges. Believes that Hawkes
intends for us to turn against the beautiful language
and desire which Cyril presents to us and to recognize
them as our own secret yearnings for a paradise which,
if attained, would only foster in us a monstrous type
of love.

299.   Forrester, Viviane. "Désastre et volupté." La Quin-
        zaine littéraire (Paris), July 16-31, 1973, pp. 13-
        4; reprinted in L'Année littéraire 1973: Choix d'-
        articles publiés par "La Quinzaine littéraire,"
        pp. 104-6. Présenté par Maurice Nadeau, Paris:
        La Quinzaine littéraire, 1974. *
        In each novel Hawkes continues to explore reality
in his own unique way, exhibiting a new field of vision, cuts and wounds and showing abrupt flashes
"d'un monde imprégné de terreur et de délices,
d'âcres, de nautres malheurs en des temps explosés"
(of a world pregnant with terror, delights, bitter happenings, and our misfortunes in explosive times). Desire and disaster abound in lines which, on the surface, suggest that all is sweetness and light and ulti-

mately paint a picture of an Illyria where an excess
of happiness through love ("du bonheur amoureux")
leads to its destruction. Hawkes's artistry--his sor-
cery--lies in his ability to create such an ambiguous
world. Read this rare work to discover the distance
between what was, and what could have been, said.

300.   Fouchet, Max-Pol. "Que dirais-tu d'un peu de vertu? "
           Le Point, October 1, 1973, pp. 96-7. +
           Presents a sympathetic interpretation of this nov-
         el, considered more readable and better controlled
         than Hawkes's other fictions and, in consequence, a
         work of the novelist's maturity. Praises Hawkes's
         treatment of the theme of the union of sex and death
         and his judicious departure at times from rhetorical
         construction to an easier, yet powerful, style. In
         closing applauds Hawkes as one of the best contempo-
         rary foreign writers and one of the best of modern
         poets.

301.   Ganz, Earl. Review of The Blood Oranges. Medi-
           terranean Review 2 (Winter 1972): 42. +
           Comparing Hawkes to the Flemish painter, Brue-
         ghel, sees in the works of both men effects resulting
         from "a certain medieval distance ... a hovering
         point of view, " and an expression of the beauty of this
         terrible world in either color (Brueghel) or in descrip-
         tion (Hawkes). Attributes weaknesses of this new nov-
         el to attempts to create less difficult works.

302.   Gros, Léon-Gabriel. "La Tapisserie rose. " Le
           Provençal Dimanche (Marseilles), August 26,
           1973, p. 8. +
           French readers, used to American writers Hem-
         ingway and Faulkner, will be taken aback by Hawkes,
         who discovers himself in his writing and whose man-
         ner of expression is at least as important as what he
         says. In this latest novel Hawkes, like Cyril, is a
         sex-singer, although eroticism is a mystical experi-
         ence for him, and "cette idylle charnelle baigne dans
         une lumière d'apocalypse" (this carnal idyll bathes in
         an apocalyptic light), seeming, in addition, to be more
         like a poem than a novel.

303.   H(all), J(oan) J(offe). "Blood Oranges is a Minor
           Masterpiece. " Houston Post, September 12, 1971,
           Spotlight section, p. 27. -

Declares the novel to be another of Hawkes's experiments in sexual pathology, "a study in lyrical decadence." Dislikes the work but realizes that it is "powerful, vivid, and haunting" and a "minor masterpiece."

304.   Henninger, Daniel. "Illyrian Idyll." National Observer, December 4, 1971, p. 24.   o
"A novelistic daredevil," whose technique includes nearly hypnotic prose, Hawkes here presents Cyril and Fiona, sex aestheticians, to enact his "theory of 'sensuous rationality'--the latitude for spouses to take lovers openly."

305.   Hill, William B.   Review of The Blood Oranges. America, November 20, 1971, p. 430.
Likely to appeal to those who appreciate the "peculiar beauties" of Hawkes's style, this novel is a "sexual satire of four people living, all too literally, together" and contains much symbolism but no chronology.

306.   "Ironizing in Illyria."   Times Literary Supplement, October 15, 1971, p. 1247.   +
Not the surreal writer that he was in The Cannibal and, therefore, not as appreciated by the young, Hawkes has created in this novel, nonetheless, a Twelfth Night which has been "gothicized with symbols, contraptions, towers and dungeons, and, of course, death." Artfully woven with "unfolding ironies," its final triumph is in its "provocative openendedness," a feature which prevents the reader from discerning the "truth or untruth of the attitudes to love the characters represent."

307.   Kennedy, William.   "The Oranges Are in the Blood, but Where Is the Blood?" Look, October 5, 1971, pp. 62-3.   *
Characterizing The Blood Oranges as an attempt "to mythologize wife-swapping" and as "one of the silliest pieces of serious literary work we are likely to get this year from a first-line American novelist," Kennedy compares it unfavorably with The Lime Twig, "one of the most perfect novels of the '60's." Also, the reviewer demonstrates the kinship of the novel to Twelfth Night and deplores what he considers an excess of symbolism and wretched use of dialogue.

308.   Kitchen, Paddy.   "Gay Edwardians."   Scotsman (Ed-
            inburgh, Scotland), October 9, 1971, Weekend
            Review section, p. 3.
        John Hawkes is "one of the superb stylists of our
period," his writing sometimes outdazzling Nabokov
in Lolita.   His latest work is a "superb erotic novel
containing no sexual athletics" but displaying exquisite
prose and "meticulously detailed set pieces."

309.   Kravitz, Philip.   "A Parody of the Confessional Novel."
            Village Voice, October 14, 1971, pp. 27-8.   *
        The black humor attained in Hawkes's difficult, un-
compromising works recalls Kafka and the later Melville, while the "hallucinatory and satiric exploration
of consciousness and reality" reminds us of Burroughs and Sontag and the stunning language, of Joyce
and Nabokov.   The novel in hand is the most accessible to date but is also the most deceptive and the-
matically challenging.   Through a "chain of disparate
images and metaphors" it parodies "courtly love, romance, and the Mediterranean mood," as well as the
confessional novel, and satirizes "the enlightened
multi-sexualist" with great skill and cunning.

310.   Las Vergnas, Raymond.   "Cris d'alarme."   Les
            Nouvelles littéraires (Paris), July 30-August 5,
            1973, p. 3.   o
        Indicating Hawkes's adoption of an anti-realist
technique using hallucination and complex construc-
tions, briefly comments on the story of this "incur-
sion onirique" (dreamlike foray) into eroticism.

311.   L(e)-C(lec'h), G(uy).   "John Hawkes: Talent con-
            firmé."   Le Figaro littéraire (Paris), September
            1, 1973, p. 3.   -
        Creator of violent, mysterious worlds, tinged
with nearly mystical elements reminiscent of D. H.
Lawrence, Hawkes here offers a novel which, with
amazing tonal restraint and use of allegory, treats
conjugal love and adultery in a satirical, yet almost
sacred, manner.   Eroticism becomes, in his hands,
"une puissance qui métamorphose l'existence" (a power which metamorphosizes existence) and sexual freedom, a conquest.

312.   Lehmann-Haupt, Christopher.   "Cyril & Fiona & Hugh
            & Cathy."   New York Times, September 15,

1971, p. 45. +
Recognizes that the novel's rich, complex language,
setting, and use of first-person narrative strive to destroy the normal moral response to what, otherwise,
would be considered a conventional story, and attempt
to render this "domestic complication" timeless. However, despite admiration of some powerful scenes and
remarks upon the work's place in Hawkes's corpus,
finds distaste for the "hip" dialogue, "beddings," and
"weight of detail."

313. Le Vot, André. Review of Les Oranges de Sang. Es-
      prit 9 (September 1973): 340-2. +
      Le Vot suggests that the inaccessibility of Hawkes's
works, along with their immersion in cruelty and horror, explains their lack of popularity. However, he
feels that this book is the most readable, since it includes simple situations, a smooth texture, the most
finished form, and "livre en filigrane certains secrets
de l'esthétique hawksienne" (displays in filigree certain
of Hawkes's aesthetic secrets), which depend on unusual use of language and time and on the choice of
setting. After describing the story, he stresses that
the somber ending should be but a starting point for
discovering the true world behind the verbal architec-
ture of the novel.

314. Loukides, Paul. "Rendezvous on a Mythical Island."
      Detroit Sunday News, November 14, 1971. p. E-
      5. -
      "A must for any reader of serious fiction," this
novel, the most accessible of Hawkes's works to date,
reveals an attitude toward human sexuality, which
"makes the much vaunted 'liberated' best sellers seem
petty and constricted." For, in the character of Cyril Hawkes has recaptured "a pagan singer of sex."

315. Lundgren, Caj. "Med Språket i Förgrunden" [Lan-
      guage in the Foreground]. Svenska Dagbladet
      (Stockholm), March 10, 1972, p. 4. +
      Lundgren reviews this novel as part of a general
article concerning the emphasis on style--or in Tony
Tanner's words, the foregrounding of language--in the
works of many contemporary American novelists.
More specifically, he speaks of Hawkes as the origi-
nator of the type of novel in which the style, by its
combination of cold detachment, grim humor, and lit-

erary beauty, sheds light on our potential for brutality and absurdity. Lundgren calls the novel in hand
a lyrical jest with undertones that shift between demonic activities and parody. He elaborates on this
statement, including most prominently, observations
on Cyril, the scenery, and the true-to-life stance of
all of the evil incidents in the book. He acknowledges, though, that the overworked style (or foregrounding of language) makes the events and characters appear unrealistic.

316.   McGuane, Thomas. Review of The Blood Oranges.
        New York Times Book Review, September 19,
        1971, p. 1; reprinted in International Herald Trib-
        une (Paris), September 24, 1971, p. 14; French
        translation by Adélaïde Blasquez, "Un Article du
        'New York Times Book Review' sur peut-être le
        meilleur écrivain américain vivant. " La Quin-
        zaine littéraire (Paris), May 1-15, 1972, pp. 11-
        2.   *
        "Feasibly our best writer, " Hawkes has produced
works of extraordinary intensity and originality, following in the footsteps of Nathanael West and Kafka.
The present book, relentlessly original and reminiscent of Twelfth Night in atmosphere and the "emul-
sive colors of Nabokov" is "a sequence of lyrical
and narrative meditations on sexual multiplicity, " with
Cyril, the narrator, infusing everything sexual with
his romantic vision. Hawkes is difficult, but after
this, his most accessible novel, if he is not widely
read, "it is no longer Hawkes who is tested. "

317.   Moran, Charles. "John Hawkes' New Novel Extends
        the Frontiers of Prose Fiction. " Brown Alumni
        Monthly 72 (January 1972): 34-5.   *
        Devoting half of his comments to the novellas of
Lunar Landscapes, calls Charivari, The Goose on the
Grave, and The Owl "comic and resonant wasteland
pieces, " the former being a mocking song which is a
"brilliant tour de force, " and The Goose on the Grave,
"Hawkes' response to Castiglione's Courtier. " Describes The Blood Oranges as a "bowl of fruit, prose
passages that are lush, sweet, poised on the thin edge
of decadence" and "Hawkes' tribute and reply to Ford
Madox Ford's The Good Soldier. " Hails it further as
a "courageous novel, " which "extends the frontiers of
prose fiction. "

318.   . "John Hawkes: Paradise Gaining." Mas-
              sachusetts Review 12 (Autumn 1971): 840-5. #
      "A comic lyric poem in prose" and one of
Hawkes's most difficult performances, this novel pays
tribute to and is a reply to Ford Madox Ford's The
Good Soldier, although the differences between the two
works are more readily seen than the similarities.
Hawkes's customary landscape, lending itself as a
"battleground between the life instinct and death instinct," here witnesses a qualified and limited victory
by the life instinct. Cyril resembles the Dionysius
described in Norman O. Brown's Love's Body and is
a "comic and slightly sinister hero," an apostle of
Eros.
      Most enjoyable is Hawkes's prose which, nonethe-
less, "places almost Jamesian demands upon the reader." Also, the reader must enjoy being outraged and
abused to appreciate the comic aspects of the work.

319. Nye, Robert. "A Man with a Secret." Manchester
      Guardian, October 14, 1971, p. 9. +
      Though a "master technician" with words, Hawkes
risks remaining a novelist's novelist if he persists in
writing with such indifference to being understood,
"like a man with a secret," much like Faulkner. Attempting an erotic novel like Updike's Couples, he
misses the latter's lightness by creating an unusually
complex narrative point of view in sentences that are
"too self-absorbed, too slow, too stately" for the subject matter.

320. Pine, John C. Review of The Blood Oranges. Li-
      brary Journal 96 (September 1, 1971): 2670-1.
      o
      Acknowledges that Hawkes is rightfully called one
of the most brilliant contemporary novelists, but confesses that this "modern fable about Illyria" puzzled
him with its "strangely diminished" terror and nearly
banal comedy.

321. Railton, Steve. "The Blood Oranges." Columbia
      Spectator (N. Y.), October 19, 1971, pp. 4-5. +
      In pointing out the similarities between Ford Mad-
ox Ford's The Good Soldier and this "brilliant ...
sensuous ... quietly moving" novel, Railton sees both
books to be about the character of the narrator, a
self-deceptive man, incapable of feeling. He also of-

fers a few comparisons with Twelfth Night with respect to setting and characterization.

322.   Review of The Blood Oranges.   Choice 9 (March
            1972): 60.
        Like the work of D. H. Lawrence in its emphasis
on atmosphere and lush description, this "highly
rhapsodic, sensual novel" evokes "a sometimes comic,
sometimes hallucinatory sense of timelessness, obsession, and escape from reality."

323.   Review of The Blood Oranges.   New Republic, No-
            vember 27, 1971, p. 29. o
        Concentrates on Cyril, the narrator, attributing
to him "nearly all the gifts of a distinguished novelist," even though his prose is overly elegant and "his
thoughts arty."

324.   Review of The Blood Oranges.   Publishers Weekly 200
            (August 16, 1971): 54.
        Written by "one of the most original and powerful
writers of contemporary fiction," this work is "a brilliant and highly effective study in eroticism that reads
at times like poetry and is possessed of very subtle
and ironic psychological insights."

325.   Review of The Blood Oranges.   Virginia Quarterly Re-
            view 48 (Winter 1972): xviii; excerpted in Con-
            temporary Literary Criticism, p. 215 (No. 586).
            o
        A pastoral prose romance, incorporating "extrav-
agant sentiments about free love" and an idyllic landscape.   However, its "pedestrian pace" lends it an
"inescapable air of dullness, characteristic of the
form."   Hawkes, nonetheless, is a highly capable literary craftsman who uses "astonishingly lyrical and
persuasive prose."

326.   Sale, Roger.   "What Went Wrong?"   New York Re-
            view of Books, October 21, 1971, pp. 3-4, 6
            [3]; excerpted in Contemporary Literary Criticism,
            p. 214-5 (No. 586).   +
        "The work of a contemptible imagination," The
Blood Oranges is "only the nightmare vision of a narrator unable to see how awful he is."   While some
may say that I have missed the fact that this novel is
a parody, I say that "when horror becomes a pastime

it should announce itself or at least know itself. "
[See also Gilbert Sorrentino's rebuttal of Sale's
point of view in a letter published in the New York
Review of Books, December 1, 1971, p. 36. Sale's
reply to Sorrentino's remarks are found in another
letter on the same page.]

327. Schott, Webster. "Philosopher of Sexistentialism. "
Life, October 8, 1971, p. [22]. +
Suggests that in this tour of the "Hawkesian
World of Enchanting Decay, " which is actually "poetry
passing as fiction [and] intellectualism doubling as sex
daydream, " we are made to feel anxious and to question "the assumptions of our intimate relationships. "
Yet concludes that Hawkes's aim is not to moralize
but to foster sensual participation, "to raise every
sensation to superawareness. "

328. Sorrentino, Gilbert. Review of The Blood Oranges.
Modern Occasions 3 (Winter 1972): 156-7. +
"I see The Blood Oranges as one of the best novels published in the country in a decade. " It is much
like Ford's The Good Soldier with respect to the narrators, Cyril and John Dowell, and the nature of the
narratives. Certainly, while some critics cannot see
that Cyril's blindness to his own awfulness is one of
the points of the novel, it is exactly "the quality of
Cyril's voice that carries the book. " Moreover, the
objective of Hawkes's novel appears to be that attainment to a terrestrial paradise is short-lived and
"must be paid for in misery and blood. "

329. Symons, Julian. "Comedy beside the Grave. " Sunday Times (London), October 10, 1971, p. 39. -
This "clash between Epicurean and Puritan views
of life, seen in specifically sexual terms, " should
have been written in a less enervating style and could
have been improved by occasional departure from
"the over-civilised attitudinising of Cyril. "

330. Tavernier, René. Review of Les Oranges de Sang.
Centre-Dimanche-Le Progrès (Saint Etienne),
July 22, 1973, p. 16; also in Le Progrès Di-
manche (Lyon), July 22, 1973, p. PR-[2].
Regards this novel as a "récit insupportablement
littéraire" (an unbearably literary narrative) which
does not convince him of Hawkes's greatness, as pro-

claimed by McGuane (No. 316).

331. Thompson, R. J.   Review of The Blood Oranges.
          Best Sellers 31 (October 1, 1971): 300; excerpted
          in Contemporary Literary Criticism, p. 214 (No.
          586).   -
      "One of the new novel's most promising phantas-
ists," Hawkes here presents a version of "Bob and
Carol and Ted and Alice," done in a "poetic cinematic
style" which involves creating "beautiful word-tapes-
tries of pure suggestion," as well as "an extra-dimen-
sional, mythical world." It demands probing and rereading until the reader understands "that all things
are connected through the power of the imagination and
memory."

332. Weales, Gerald.   "Fiction Chronicle." Hudson Review
          24 (Winter 1971/72): 716-30. [728-30] *
      Sketchily describes the story and landscape of the
novel.   Thereafter, concentrates on the book's comic
design, which appears to depend on "our recognizing
and responding to a disagreement between Cyril and
his creator about which of the quaternion [the four
main characters] is the 'real' one." Holds Cyril to
be so tiresome, though, that if we take this character
and his pronouncements seriously, "the novel would
lose its sustaining value."

333. Weigel, John A.   "Matters of the Heart." Cincinnati
          Enquirer, September 16, 1971, p. 69. +
      In the tradition of Colette and Proust this is "a
story with charm and poignancy [woven] out of the
crass theme of sexual infidelity--including enough ex-
plicitness for honesty but not so much as to attract
the merely prurient." Perhaps time will tell us more
about the credibility of this novel.

334. West, Ray B.   "Fancy and Impassioned Courage."
          San Francisco Fault, November 10, 1971, pp.
          20-1. *
      Focuses on Hawkes's heroes, men of "fancy and
impassioned courage," whose main purpose is to portray the novelist's feeling that the world is "an absurd struggle to achieve total identity" and to promote
his fictional vision reflecting a "yearning after something lost." Believing that in all except The Blood
Oranges Hawkes's overriding concern has been for

the nature of heroism, explains his perception of this
concern in several of the novels. Also suggests that
in The Blood Oranges the emphasis is on demonstrating the perils and pleasures of marriage and sexual
love. Concludes by speculating about the differences
in the novel, had Hugh been the "hero."

335.   Willis, Judy. Review of The Blood Oranges. Wood-
            wind 3 (February 22, 1972): 12.   *
        "If The Blood Oranges is not a best-seller, it will
not be because it is too esoteric, but because it is too
good," since the taste of the general public leans more
towards such amateurish works as The Exorcist.   The
point of view of Cyril, the "sex-singer," is the essence of the novel--a point of view expressed in "the
languid language of exotic eroticism a little like Lawrence Durrell's." Also like Durrell's Alexandria
Quartet is the "slow unfolding of reality," accom-
plished by repeated flashbacks and flashforwards by
Hawkes.

336.   Woolley, Bryan. "A 'Sexual Dracula'." Louisville
            Courier-Journal, October 24, 1971, sec. F, p. 5.
            -
        Hawkes, "one of America's best--and least read
--novelists," is concerned in this latest work with
"the effects of sexual attitudes and life-styles on human personalities and relationships--and vice versa."
The characters are astoundingly complex and complete,
especially Cyril, "a sexual Dracula," who smilingly
destroys others while escaping all injury himself.

SEE ALSO: Nos. 339, 368, 417, 420, 422, 433, 445.

Death, Sleep & the Traveler

337.   Allen, Bruce. Review of Death, Sleep & the Travel-
            er. Library Journal 99 (June 1, 1974): 1564.
        While the novel exhibits an "inventive wealth of
detail" and "vivid entangling word pictures," its inner
meanings are enigmatic--perhaps, even private--and
it nearly disintegrates when "Hawkes reaches for narrative momentum."

338.   Amis, Martin. "Tour de Farce." New Statesman,
            February 21, 1975, p. 250.   -

It is necessary to dismiss this novel "as a bathetic and entirely risible prose-poem on the ménage à trois." one wonders if Hawkes has no ear for dialogue, can't characterise, and can't punctuate or parse. He is not "a Writer's Writer so much as a Bad Writers' Writer."

339.   Beaudot, William J. K.   Review of Death, Sleep & the Traveler.   Librarian's Choice 32 (July 1, 1974): [1]-[4].   *
Beaudot views this work as "yet another port of call on Hawkes's psychic fishing expedition" of twenty-five years.   He finds the novel to be accessible on the superficial level, yet unique in its probing of the "nether regions of 'sleep', " with Allert, the narrator as the dreamer.   Pointing out the variance between Allert's inner and outer selves, he emphasizes the necessity of questioning Allert's grasp of reality.   He concludes that as in Second Skin and in The Blood Oranges, this book has the sensual mind as its keystone and is a further attempt to shed "more light in the dark and often impenetrable corridors of mind and soul."

340.   Bedient, Calvin.   "On Cat Feet."   New Republic, April 20, 1974, pp. 26-8; excerpted in Contemporary Literary Criticism, pp. 215-6 (No. 586).   +
Highly praises this "esthetic performance of the first order."   Summarizes the action although stating that far from being a normal narrative, the story is "refracted from dozens of disjunct anecdotes as if from the shattered glass face of a clock."   While lauding the novel's language, laments the detachment of the narrative, and says that Hawkes's coldness to life amounts to a punishment of it.   Maintains, finally, that in this "beautiful achievement" the novelist dwells not only on sexual guilt but also on "the guilt of the artist as such."

341.   Betsky, Celia.   "Author in Search of a Myth."   Nation, May 18, 1974, pp. 630-1; excerpted in Contemporary Literary Criticism, p. 217 (No. 586).   *
Asserting that most of Hawkes's stories have death, sleep, and travel as underlying motifs, calls Allert's voyage a "trip through disillusion and disgust" with the ports of call standing as "symbols for

aspects of his [Allert's] own life." Declares that
though violence and the memory of World War II do
not play an important part in this novel, a sexual
war--"strangely empty and mechanical"--is found instead.   Charges, too, that while Hawkes here delves
into questions of insanity, reminding us of his former
surrealism, his emphasis on searching out new dreams
for Allert and a myth for himself results in flat characters and a heartless style.

342. Blakeston, Oswell. "Fantasies, Wisecracks." Trib-
         une (London), February 14, 1975, p. 7. o
      Analyzes briefly the character Allert and his prob-
lems and stands amazed at Hawkes's talent in articu-
lating the sensual mind as found in the story's narrator.   Understands how people can feel irritated by
such a fantasy but states that for him the novel is
haunting, and is "the fabled track to the bedroom of
a Dutchman with psychic sores."

343. Blumberg, Myrna. Review of Death, Sleep & the
         Traveler. Times (London), February 20, 1975,
         p. 12.
      "Confirms this writer's skill at being seriously
shaking in lyrical sentences."

344. Brode, Anthony. "Incest and Knickers." Southern
         Evening Echo (Southampton, England), February
         13, 1975, p. 13. [Column signed: Tom Brode]
      Written in an elegant style, this book is experi-
enced as a series of highly erotic dreams.   Yet
Hawkes appears to catch "something of the sinuous
movement of underwater vegetation" in his style and
spends much of his time peering at it.

345. Bromwich, David. Review of Death, Sleep & the
         Traveler. New York Times Book Review, April
         21, 1974, pp. 5-6; excerpted in Contemporary
         Literary Criticism, p. 216 (No. 586),   +
      Hawkes, "a prince of the middle-aged avant-
garde," has grown in reputation in recent years.   However, his present effort is a "vasty dreamy arty mythy
set piece of reverie," which contains too high a per-
centage of cant, and, as is the case with his works in
general, reveals its thinness and its foundation upon
"naive modernism."   Saul Bellow and Flannery O'Connor perhaps like Hawkes because "they sense he is

trying to do much that they have succeeded in doing.
Surely, Hawkes has the rhythms of a great novelist
but not the revelations, the cunning required to be a
great prose stylist without the calling. "
[See also No. 71 for Hawkes's reply to Bromwich's statement about Flannery O'Connor's estimation of his work.]

346.   Brooks, Jeremy. "Captured by Dreams." Sunday
       Times (London), February 16, 1975, p. 38.   -
       Speculates first about Ursula's reason for leaving
Allert and then confesses that Hawkes's work "almost
defies review, for no category would hold him. "
Firmly denies that the novel is either poetic or symbolic and declares that after considerable thought he
cannot yet discover the reason for his intense enjoyment of the work.

347.   Brooks, Michael. "A Novelist's Private Landscape. "
       Baltimore Sun, April 21, 1974, p. D-7.   +
       Always Hawkes's novels have been like symbolist
poems in construction and have evidenced his "magnificent descriptive gift. " His recent works, though
more accessible than earlier ones, nonetheless are
confusing and disturbing, as well as fascinating. The
present novel is skilfully done, but we are not sure
what is meant to be funny or "where mockery leaves
off and seriousness begins. " We discover that cow-
ardice is Allert's problem; Hawkes's style is ours.

348.   Broyard, Anatole. "Having at the Avant-garde. "
       New York Times, April 11, 1974, p. 33; also as
       a Review of Death, Sleep & the Traveler, Inter-
       national Herald Tribune (Paris), April 24, 1974,
       p. 14.   +
       This novel is "remorseless ... in its original-
ity, " being an example of the trend in American fiction towards a new kind of symbolism, according to
which "everything sounds laboriously thought up or out
and means both more than meets the eye and less than
meets the mind. " Moreover, as the reader can see
from the book, it is a pretentious work with omnipres-
ent "dread, mysterical" metaphors, no character development or plot, and a narrator who speaks in
"stilted polysyllables. "

349.   Bruni, Thomas G. Review of Death, Sleep & the

Traveler. <u>Lehigh Valley Labor Herald</u> (Allentown, Pa.), May 3, 1974, p. 7. o
Challenging, but "tantalizingly elusive," this novel
is superb in its "supple prose" and "brilliant images"
that "often stop the reader in his tracks."

350.   [Brussat, Frederic A.] "Eroscope & Dreamscape."
       <u>Cultural Information Service</u> 5 (May 1974): 12-
       3. +
       Offers comments on Hawkes, along with remarks
on Carol Hill's <u>Let's Fall in Love</u>, and interjects in
several places quotations from various people concerning the ideas presented. With respect to Hawkes,
informs us that this novelist was the first to "write
novels with closed structures," in which the main focus is on language, atmosphere, and tone. States,
too, that Hawkes uses dreamscapes to organize his
fictional elements and to illuminate "the schemes,
feelings, beliefs which may be locked in our unconscious minds." Asserts that in <u>Death, Sleep & the
Traveler</u> both closed structure and dreamscape are
evident and that the reader should not be frustrated
by its poetic language and jumbled narration.

351.   C(abau), J(acques). "Hawkes: Jeu de cartes scab-
       reux." <u>L'Express</u>, April 21-27, 1975, p. 40. o
       Like Mandiargues, Hawkes steadfastly parades
"situations scabreuses sous le soleil noir du surréal-
isme" (improper situations under the black sun of
surrealism). Here he has produced, above all, a
detective story which explores "la fatale liaison de
l'amour et de la mort" (the fatal relationship between
love and death). Its disconnected scenes remind us
of an improper card game, in which no matter how
hard he tries, the reader can never win, and Hawkes
alone knows the secret.

352.   Carriere, Bennett. Review of <u>Death, Sleep & the
       Traveler</u>. <u>Minnesota Daily</u> (Minneapolis), June
       24, 1975, p. 8. *
       Using Ortega y Gasset's analogy between novel
writing and mining a quarry, contends that Hawkes
"has found a vein that is rich if not wide." States
that Hawkes's rejection of plot and structure persists
in this novel but that also mood, atmosphere, and especially ambiance maintain their key positions. Can-
didly notes that the book "eludes my analysis based

upon 'sense','" while praising the novelist's rhythmic prose by quoting Allert's description of drinking water.

353.   Cohen, George. "The Sleepless Dreams of John
        Hawkes." Chicago Tribune, April 14, 1974,
        Book World section, p. 1.   +
        Exclaiming that this is "an exquisite novel by a
very gifted novelist," notes generally Hawkes's creation of dream landscapes, use of recurring images,
and appeals to the senses. Refers briefly to several
earlier works by the novelist and then describes the
story of the present novel, a work "filled with Allert's dreams."

354.   Corwin, Phillip. Review of Death, Sleep & the Trav-
        eler. National Observer, July 20, 1974, p. 21.
        -
        "John Hawkes is a writer of dazzling talent and
subtle wit," whose method includes mixing myth and
reality and using "visceral" imagery and cinematic
techniques. Yet, in trying "to portray despair, decadence, and death" in this work he has toned down his
writing, resulting in unconvincing narrative and dull
eroticism. In addition, the novel's message, that life
is hopeless and personal satisfaction is "totally unob-
tainable," undermines the book.

355.   "Du cote des grands." Résonance-La Vie Lyonnaise
        (Lyon), February 28, 1975, p. 45. o
        Don't read this book too hastily! For you will
miss Hawkes's unusual gift for putting into words
"les rêves, les illusions, les fausses évasions et les
chimères" (dreams, illusions, false escapes, chime-
ras)--elements which are apt to undo mankind.

356.   Duranteau, Josane. "Psychiatres de romans."
        L'Education, no. 243 (April 24, 1975), pp. 28-9.
        -
        "Ce roman évoque un enfer" (This novel evokes a
kind of hell). Its haphazard sequence of scenes and
wild leaps from one theme to another, as I have il-
lustrated here, suggest decay ("une décomposition").
Moreover, it is a sick dream, in which there is no
love and no communication beyond that of the flesh
among the characters.

357. Eron, Carol. "Prisoner of the Self." Washington
      Post, May 26, 1974, Book World section, p. 3;
      also as "As We Turn from Truth." Boston Sun-
      day Globe, July 14, 1974, p. 49; excerpted in
      Contemporary Literary Criticism, p. 218 (No.
      586).   +
      Hawkes's brief novel is "a series of exquisitely
      drawn, fragmented episodes ... that together create
      the effect of a collection of photographs ... some
      sharply focused, others faded or shadowy or dissolved
      in brilliant light." Its frequent images and symbols
      linger in the mind, and the highly-stylized prose,
      sometimes humorous, sometimes enchanting, is "al-
      ways sensual and evocative." Allert variously states
      the theme as "the 'destructive nature of the uncon-
      scious ... sensual isolation' " or the articulation of
      the sensual mind. But the emotional impact of the
      book comes from the loneliness of Allert, "the pris-
      oner of self."

358. Fleury, Claude. "Joyce Carol Oates: 'Le Pays des
      merveilles'." Le Republicain Lorrain (Metz,
      France), March 2, 1975, p. [25].
      Merely a few words on Hawkes's new work, indi-
      cating that like The Blood Oranges its activities take
      place in an unreal world.

359. Frohock, W. M. "How Hawkes's Humor Works."
      Southwest Review 59 (Summer 1974): 330-2; ex-
      cerpted in Contemporary Literary Criticism, pp.
      218-9 (No. 586), although erroneously ascribed
      to David Dillon in that work.   +
      Mainly reviews Greiner's Comic Terror: the Nov-
      els of John Hawkes (No. 578) and agrees with Greiner's
      feeling that Hawkes's recent novels have been more
      accessible than his earlier works. However, finds
      that Hawkes's fictions are now disconcerting the reader
      far too little and that Death, Sleep & the Traveler
      lacks grotesqueness in the proper amounts and the
      "good old oneiric atmosphere."

360. Gatling, Frank. "A Middle-aged Man at the Apex of
      Two Triangles." Washington Star, April 28,
      1974, p. G-3.   +
      Admiring Hawkes's mastery of "slowly revealing
      attitude through snatches of dialogue" and his charac-
      terization through "minutely recorded actions and ob-

servations of the protagonist-narrator," Gatling, on
the other hand, is disturbed by the novelist's water-
ing-down of his "brilliant descriptive quality," resulting in a loss of his former forceful poetic imagery,
to obtain greater clarity in his two latest works. He
recommends Hawkes's present work but claims that it
is a "pathetic" comedy, whose "scenes are comic,
but not funny" and that Hawkes could have produced
a better novel.

361.   Gelfant, Blanche. "Chronicles and Chroniclers: Some
        Contemporary Fictions." Massachusetts Review
        16 (Winter 1975): 127-43. [130-3] *
        Disorder reigns in the world of this novel, with
hallucination, nightmare, coma, and trance turning its
characters into "grotesques, horrifying, comic, and
finally unfathomable." Recurring actions, essential to
Hawkes's works, lend the work a dream-like effect,
while the plotlessness, allowing the unexpected, becomes ominous. Verbal, psychological, and imagistic
coherence occurs but only helps to suspend the meaning of the novel. Since the real issues are never
clear, a heavy comic overtone arises, inducing anxiety.

362.   Gleick, James. "Waking to Sleep." Harvard Crim-
        son, April 27, 1974, p. 2. +
        "America's least-read major novelist" has been
creating largely plotless, but still turbulent, works recently. In this latest novel real movement, in fact,
occurs only "through the depths of Allert's consciousness," and contributes to the fact that the other characters are never really developed and Ursula, for example, is little more than a parody. Nonetheless,
Hawkes "demonstrates tight-rope delicacy in bringing
off the most predictable of metaphors" and turns the
sequence of vignettes into a novel by adding an undercurrent of terror.

363.   Green, Randall. Review of Death, Sleep & the Travel-
        er. Village Voice, May 23, 1974, p. 37; excerpt-
        ed in Contemporary Literary Criticism, pp. 271-8
        (No. 586). +
        Judges this work to be a depthless, "academic ex-
ercise," containing but a few powerful images and re-
vealing that Hawkes's attempt to create "a world surreal and ordinary at the same time," in the manner of

Nabokov, has not succeeded. Criticizes the novelist
for his "falsely ambiguous style" and for failing to
clothe his literary devices with some shape and meaning.

364. Halio, Jay L. "Love and the Grotesque." Southern
      Review n. s. 11 (October 1975): 942-8. [942-4]
      +
      Maintains that Hawkes's newest novel, an "excel-
lent sequel to his celebrated Blood Oranges," continues the novelist's preoccupation with "sexual myth
and fantasy, and their relation to our real lives."
Shows Hawkes's obsession with the grotesque also in
several examples from the book.

365. Harrison-Ford, Carl. "Every Man Is an Island."
      Sydney (Australia) Morning Herald, July 19, 1975,
      Weekend Magazine section, p. 18.   +
      "One of Hawkes' most beautifully formed and care-
fully structured novels," this work really concerns itself with our travels "simultaneously towards death
and understanding" and promotes the concept that
"self-knowledge leads to isolation," brought about by
"the death of others and our knowledge of our own
mortality." Moreover, it is a book which acquires
greater immediacy through its complex structuring.
Certainly, too, Hawkes controls his symbols and narrative wholly and has triumphed by emphasizing tone
and control rather than characterization. He is "one
of the most underated [sic] of contemporary novelists."

366. Hills, Rust. "Writing." Esquire, July 1974, pp.
      42, 44, 49. [42, 49] o
      Having always considered Hawkes too difficult to
read, Hills expresses surprise at this short, often
times funny, and quite likable offering. He specifically notes the "constant suggestion of a dream" in
Hawkes's writing and the very luxuriant language of
these dreamlike features.

367. Juin, Hubert. "Les Rêves allégoriques de John
      Hawkes." Le Monde (Paris), March 14, 1975,
      p. 21. +
      Intertwining dreams and broken narrative, the
novel gives us another glimpse of Hawkes's fictive
world--"ce climat pesant mais dansant qui glisse à

chaque seconde vers le cauchemar" (this heavy but
dancing climate which slips second by second towards
nightmare). By combining everyday and unreal experiences with allegorical dreams so that the differences between sleeping and waking, real and imaginary events, and death and love are not discernible,
Hawkes succeeds in enclosing us, as well as Allert,
in an inescapable world of fantasy, overflowing with
sensual images.

368.   Koch, Stephen. "Circling Hawkes." Saturday Re-
           view/World, June 1, 1974, pp. 20-2. #
        In describing Hawkes's early method of writing,
points out his continual experimentation with the novel
form while others were turning to realism, and suggests that Hawkes's use of a new kind of violence was
a result of his wartime experiences. Discusses The
Beetle Leg, which he considers "the only great American surrealist novel." However, with Second Skin
notices a shift in focus from Hawkes's "haunted con-
structs of terror" to "a more ventilated, linear story
line, where the main energy was no longer phantasma-
goric but erotic." Fascinated by Second Skin, yet un-
impressed with The Blood Oranges, finally voices dis-
appointment with the present work, saying that it is
intensely sexual but "virtually all narrative line and
little else."

369.   Kosek, Steven. "Reticular Prose, Visceral Effects."
           St. Louis Post-Dispatch, May 5, 1974, p. 4-D.
           o
        Exhibiting an overpowering style and leaving large-
ly inexpressible impressions, Hawkes's novels also
bear themes which "must be absorbed as a series of
sensations that easily by-pass the intellectual circuit-
ry." Central to the newest work are Allert's re-
sponses to "two tri-part relationships."

370.   Las Vergnas, Raymond. "Alcools." Les Nouvelles
           littéraires (Paris), April 28-May 4, 1975, p. 6.
           -
        Outlines the action of the novel for the most part
but remarks also that in all of his works Hawkes creates a dreamlike atmosphere, "qui transmue ses héros
en la synthèse des ombres qui le hantent, et rien
d'autre" (which transforms the hero into nothing more
than a synthesis of the shadows which haunt him), and

throughout which spirits, love, death, and solitude are
woven.

371.   Le Clec'h, Guy. "Exister grâce à la sexualité."
          Le Figaro littéraire (Paris), March 29-30, 1975,
          p. 16. +
          Likening Hawkes's novels to burning icebergs,
says that in each work the obvious elements, such as
characters and style, "repose sur une part de l'être
human invisible, explosive, ses rêves, sa sexualité"
(are based on the invisible, explosive aspects of the
human being--his dreams and his sexuality). In an
interview with the novelist elicits comments on Death,
Sleep & the Traveler, including the fact that Hawkes
sees the novel as a work based largely on dreams,
containing comedy, comments on existence and sexuality, and the thought that everyone is capable of murder.

372.   Le Vot, André. "John Hawkes à la recherche d'une
          totalité perdue." La Quinzaine littéraire (Paris),
          March 16-31, 1975, pp. 9-10. *
          With this novel Hawkes tries to isolate and define
"le facteur central, l'aliénation qui marque la plupart
de ses personnages" (the central factor, the alienation
which marks most of his characters). There is evidence of the same quest for a lost wholeness ("une
totalité perdue"), which The Cannibal displays, but
here the emphasis falls on the pathological character
of the splintering, uncommunicative civilization presented.
          Reports, after a short summary of the novel, sev-
eral interchanges during an interview with the novelist. The remarks concern the origin of the title for
Death, Sleep & the Traveler, and of the basic idea
for the book, a comparison of Cyril, Allert, and the
narrator of Travesty, and the alternation of scenes in
some of the novels, including The Cannibal and
Hawkes's latest.

373.   _____. "Une Vision apocalyptique du monde." Le
          Quotidien de Paris, March 7, 1975, p. 11. *
          Enumerates all of the constants of Hawkes's works,
including the apocalyptic vision, dreamlike landscape,
terror, and a decaying universe which leaves the individual "dans une effroyable solitude, face aux prob-
lèmes élémentaires de la survie" (frightfully alone to

face the elementary problems of survival). Yet discovers in the present novel a forcefulness stemming
from the apparent peacefulness of its central situation
--the impossibility of Allert's assuming a second skin.
     In interviewing Hawkes, though concentrating on
the structure and meaning of the new novel, succeeds
in learning, too, that the novelist believes that all of
his novels together form a generalized metaphor of
his conception of the human condition.

374.   Lothamer, Eileen.   Review of Death, Sleep & the Trav-
              eler.   Long Beach Press-Telegram, April 24,
              1974, p. P-6; also in Long Beach Independent, Ap-
              ril 25, 1974, p. Z-3.   -
         Not an "easy read," this novel fascinates us with
         its "conscious artistry" and "manipulations of myth
         and imagery." It is a thought-provoking work, in
         which "Allert's life-dream-life visions vibrate far be-
         yond the plot."

375.   McCabe, Carol.   "Tight As a Diamond."   Providence
              Sunday Journal, May 5, 1974, Leisure Weekly sec-
              tion, p. H-19.   +
         Believes that like other contemporary surrealist
         writers Hawkes creates novels in which "ideas awakened
         in the reader's consciousness are as important as those
         in the writer's head." Feels that the pages of this
         novel are "as tightly made as a diamond," and sug-
         gests several slow readings to acquire a good under-
         standing of it and to appreciate its stunningly clear
         language.   Notes the book's sensual opulence and sev-
         eral layers of meaning, along with its puzzlement and
         terror.

376.   McCartney, Maris.   "Swopping All Round."   Glasgow
              (Scotland) Herald, February 13, 1975, p. 5.   o
         A novel with a "weirdly compelling atmosphere,"
         in which the characters lack distinctive personalities
         but are sharply defined "as examples of human psychol-
         ogy." Hawkes's writing is sensuous, poetic, and lan-
         guidly graceful.

377.   McKinley, James.   "For Hawkes, It Happens in the
              Mind--But Whose?"   Kansas City Star, May 26,
              1974, p. 3-E.   *
         Compares Hawkes's work, in general, to a rain-
         forest flower, "its fragile stem, improbable foliage,

surmounted by a strange blazing blossom," while hold-
ing Death, Sleep, & the Traveler as a "triumphant
American nouveau roman--our familiar psychological
novel mutated to a solitary narrator's mind playing on
the events, real or fancied, of his existence." Recognizes that the central idea of the novel is "Allert--
Hawkes's principle that in the urge toward sex lies,
actually and metaphorically, the purpose and end of existence." Though stating that Hawkes's brilliant style
and "formidable psychological insights" make Allert's
ceaseless attempt to explore his own mind a worth-
while fictional experience, expresses relief in escaping from Allert's confining world at the book's end.

378. MacNamee, John. "Unique View." Hartford Courant,
June 9, 1974, p. 22-F. -
Indicates the usual Hawkesian techniques found in
this novel--the surreal landscape, lack of plot, unique
imagery "that illuminates forbidden areas in our own
minds," and episodes based on a view of the world
as comic, yet terrifying. Expresses regret that its
greater accessibility means loss of some of its possible power of mystery and ranks it below Second Skin
in effectiveness.

379. Malin, Irving. Review of Death, Sleep & the Traveler. Commonweal, May 3, 1974, pp. 221-2; excerpted in Contemporary Literary Criticism, p.
217 (No. 586). +
After prefacing his remarks on this work with
statements concerning Hawkes's aims in writing fiction
and the novelist's style, Malin describes the action of
the novel, which he calls Hawkes's "most brilliant
achievement" in many ways. He sees the book as a
"philosophical thriller," "a maze-like work about
maze-like reality," and praises its unique construction, recurring, brilliant images, and its success in
provoking a cleansing anxiety in the reader.

380. Mason, Michael. "Unhappy Wanderer." Times Literary Supplement, February 14, 1975, p. 156. +
Analyzes "half-heartedly," but with much criticism,
Hawkes's "oblique and selective treatment of 'scenes'"
and use of descriptive detail and images before presenting the novel's "thin storyline of a conventional
type." Explores the implications of the parallelism
indicated by the arrangement of the book's sections

and notes the use of the Flying Dutchman legend.
Casts a closing verdict that the novel is a "bloodless,
mannered, and laconic piece of writing," which had
possibilities of form and content that were "coyly
evaded."

381.   Mellors, John.   "Humming and Whoring."   Listener,
            February 20, 1975, pp. 253-4.   [254] o
        A fictional work which includes scenes of a pre-
Raphaelite quality and through which Hawkes's intensity of vision and sharpness of observation hypnotize
the reader.   Its moral?   Possibly, that "guilt can be
a source of strength: we destroy it at our peril."

·382.   Nesbitt, W. J.   "Fiction."   Northern Echo (Darling-
            ton, England), February 14, 1975, p. 6.
        A "poetic and strangely foreign American novel,"
which is a humorless and solemn "presentation of
dreams and the experience of life, death, and sex."

383.   Nicol, Charles.   "In the Dream."   National Review,
            June 7, 1974, pp. 659-60; excerpted in Contempo-
            rary Literary Criticism, p. 218 (No. 586).   +
        "Experimental, dreamlike, sensuous, comic, and
solid," Hawkes's novels, written with "dizzying brilliance," "burn like ... a forest of sandalwood on the
hearth of the intellect."   Especially remarkable in
this novel are the dreams that seem real, surpassing
even the "past masters of the evocative dream, Nabokov and Ingmar Bergman," as well as "the reality that
seems a dream."   Sometimes Hawkes's solely symbolic images are forced, but his "comic sensuality is the
product of an Apollonian mind and a Dionysian sensi-
bility."

384.   Nolan, Tom.   "Intimate Lightning and Other Close-
            ups."   Coast Magazine 15 (June 1974): 18-9.   o
        This is "the most enjoyable novel I've read since
Thomas McGuane's Ninety-Two in the Shade" and is "a
wonderful montage of scenes drenched in a restrained,
sustained eroticism that leaves the reader gasping for
succor....   The ideas make possible the tale, but the
story is its own reward."

385.   O., P. N.   "Triangles."   Evening Post & Chronicle
            (Wigan, Lancashire, England), February 22, 1975,
            p. 7.

"Carefully constructed and stylish, Mr. Hawkes'
latest book should increase his reputation among ad-
dicts of the modern psychological, soul-searching
novel. "

386.   Oates, Quentin.   "Critics Crowner. " Bookseller, no.
       3609 (February 22, 1975), pp. 1458, 1460. +
       Criticizing reviews written by academics ("dons"),
       Oates uses as examples reviews of Death, Sleep &
       the Traveler by Lorna Sage (see no. 397) and Michael
       Mason (see no. 380).   He balances their negative re-
       actions to the novel with a few favorable quotations
       from the reviews of Jeremy Brooks (see No. 346) and
       Michael Maxwell Scott (see no. 399).

387.   Perkins, Michael.   "Swappers at Sea. " Screw, June
       24, 1974, p. 21. +
       Proclaims that Hawkes, possessing an erotic vi-
       sion similar to that of Georges Bataille, has produced
       "erotic masterpieces" with The Blood Oranges and
       Death, Sleep & the Traveler.   Touching upon the pres-
       ent novel's story and the book's hypnotic effect, notes
       that the dominant theme is sexual, and obsessively so.
       Believes that Hawkes "writes from a sickness and ob-
       session" but "opens our eyes and souls to a vision of
       sexuality unequalled in its terror. "

388.   Pickett, Rex.   Review of Death, Sleep & the Traveler.
       Los Angeles Free Press, December 16, 1974, p.
       16. +
       Hawkes's works, delicately poetic and so impor-
       tant and readable in this crazy era of ours, show con-
       stant concern with the "complex features and subtle
       outlines" of psychological depth, based on the leitmo-
       tifs of "polygamy, multi-valued and multi-valenced
       personalities, and a deep desirous auto-eroticism. "
       This new book, more profound than the novelist's
       earlier fictions, presents psychic depths pervaded by
       "polyvalence of the imagination," promoted by the de-
       vice of fragmented storytelling, and a theme which
       concerns the "Eros/Psyche myth ... the auto-erotic
       sensuality ... the perversities ... and the constant
       mythologizing of everything, mostly sex. "

389.   Plung, Daniel.   "A Story of Mixed-up Love and In-
       trigue. " Idaho Statesman, May 19, 1974, sec.
       C, p. 11. -

Delineating briefly how Hawkes's novels have become less complicated over the years, Plung judges
this novel to be the most accessible and most enjoyable while still maintaining the typical Hawkesian
features of "deaths, mysterious occurrences, and an
undercurrent of psychological intrigue."

390. Pons, Anne. "Deux trios pour un homme seul." Le
      Point, April 21, 1975, p. 154. +
      The most perfected of Hawkes's works, this novel
displays "son ardente gravité, sa magie poétique, ses
rêves éclairant le réel, sa mélopée sensuelle" (his fi-
ery seriousness, poetic magic, dreams illuminating
reality, and sensual, repetitive chanting). With quick,
syncopated rhythms and superrealistic snapshots of
reality, it works out a journey through metaphysical
insecurity and sexual anxiety. Surely, love has never
been "plus éclatant, plus lascif, plus mélodieux, plus
immortel" (more dazzling, lascivious, melodious, and
immortel), except in Sappho. Moreover, like love and
music, this book and others by Hawkes depend on har-
mony and cast spells.

391. Review of Death, Sleep & the Traveler. Booklist 70
      (May 1, 1974): 977.
      "Nostalgic reveries are intermingled with and in-
terrupted by present encounters, and the chimera of
the past is reincarnated into contemporary ordeal as
obsession is realized and transformed."

392. Review of Death, Sleep & the Traveler. Choice 11
      (July/August 1974): 759. o
      In this "most sexual" of Hawkes's novels the nov-
elist continues to emphasize the "exploration of the
conscious and unconscious sensibilities of the characters" more than the action and the presentation of
events--in prose rhythms and symbols evocative of
haunting images--more than the events themselves.

393. Review of Death, Sleep & the Traveler. Kirkus Re-
      views 42 (February 15, 1974): 203. o
      Decrying Allert's obscene sexuality, charges that
the plot is pointless and the writing, which formerly
mixed dream with past and present in an exciting
manner, "now seems designed merely to circumvent
the difficulties of narrative continuity."

394.   Review of Death, Sleep & the Traveler. Virginia
        Quarterly Review 50 (Autumn 1974): cxx.
        At times surrealistic, this is "a psychological
study with symbolic overtones," which is "absorbing,
challenging, imaginative, and to a degree mystifying."

395.   Richardson, Jean. "New Fiction." Birmingham
        (England) Post, February 22, 1975, Saturday Mag-
        azine section, p. 2.
        "The style is marvellous," ... but are the sex,
saunas, snow, and dreams "really the stuff of a masterpiece or elaborate contrivances with not much inside?"

396.   Rudden, Kevin G. "Death, Sleep & the Traveler."
        Brown Daily Herald, May 16, 1974, p. 6.   +
        Reflecting upon an interview with Hawkes, de-
scribes the novelist as quite confident and undaunted
by bad reviews of this work.   Admits not fully understanding the novel but marks the greater importance of
the presentation of the narrative over the plot and the
striking use of language.   Wonders, finally, if it is
not really Hawkes who says "I am not guilty" at the
novel's end in defense of his work.

397.   Sage, Lorna. "Eavesdropping." Observer (London),
        February 16, 1975, p. 30.   +
        A continuation of Hawkes's "erotic travelogue"
and "a sort of endless saga of eavesdropping," this
novel once again presents a hero who serves as the
watcher through whose eyes the reader and writer
view the activities of the story's "energetic lovers."
Allert's studied and ominous mental images, "caught
and held between fascination and repulsion," give life
to the narrative while the style creates practically a
lewd effect by its captivation of energies from the
world of sensation.

398.   Schwartz, Joseph. "Which Is the Real Story?" Mil-
        waukee Journal, May 12, 1974, part 5, p. 4.   -
        After suggesting three possible interpretations of
the novel, chooses the third as probably the correct
one: that Allert is insane and is inventing the whole
narrative.   Admires Hawkes's originality but misses
some of the trademarks of normal fiction.

399.   Scott, Michael Maxwell. "Recent Fiction." Daily

Telegraph (London), February 13, 1975, p. 12.
Marvelously written, but quite paradoxical, the
novel "attempts to conjure a myth of a modern man
with no spiritual centre, only a sensualism refined by
references to a Jungian psyche."

400.   Seymour-Smith, Martin.   "Victims Who Survive."
       Financial Times (London), February 27, 1975,
       0. 32.   o
       Though an original writer and successful here in
       portraying Allert with "power and linguistic appropri-
       ateness," Hawkes, in general, often uses "pointless
       violence and rhetoric" and, in this case, defeats co-
       herence with his mannered and contrived "psychiatric
       material."

401.   Silverblatt, Michael.   "Our Weekly Reader."   Spec-
       trum (S. U. N. Y.), April 12, 1974, p. 5.   *
       Dubs Hawkes "the most interesting and most sing-
       ular novelist writing today," creator of fiction evoking
       "the madness of one's worst nightmares coming relent-
       lessly true."   Recognizes the divorce of Hawkes's in-
       vented environments from normal moral and ethical
       values and his range of emotional climates from sex-
       ual sterility to cruel sensuality.   However, judges
       that Hawkes's usual brand of comedy tends towards
       boring solipsism and, ultimately, calls the book a
       "peculiar failure" due, in part, to the novelist's
       "needless interiority and ambiguity of intention."

402.   Simon, Jeff.   "Latter Day Hawkes: Neither Confused
       Nor Confusing."   Buffalo Evening News, June 8,
       1974, p. 12-C.   +
       Two years ago Hawkes gave a reading in which he
       poked fun at a "young Australian academic" who had
       noted that his work had progressed over the years
       from "dark, schizoid, experimental Gothicism" to "a
       warm, flamboyant, continuing chronicle of the flesh."
       But the novelist's fiction does show a gradual change
       from work to work, and this last book is beautiful,
       smoothly-flowing, sensual, and erotic but, like a Ma-
       tisse nude, is not in the least obscene.   Though em-
       ploying much luxurious description, the poetic prose
       is clear and direct.   It is an extraordinary work
       which will be recognized easily as such.

403.   Smith, James M.   "With-it Novel Involves Reader."

Nashville Tennessean, May 5, 1974, p. 10-F. -
In describing this "clearly significant" story,
whose world "resembles our own too closely for comfort," notes Allert's cold, detached life and lack of a
"redeeming comic vision." Thinks a failure Hawkes's
search for "a new metaphor for the condition of modern man" but lauds the book's coherence and magnificent prose.

404.   Somers, Dermot. "Egodentity and Icentricity." Irish
        Times (Dublin), February 20, 1975, p. 8. -
        Calls Hawkes's approach to exposing the workings
of human nature through "psychopoetical analysis" lyr-
ically sensitive but suspects that the novelist's talent
may be exposed as "a hollow wreath of words" once
its dependence on vapidity is shown. Here designates
the dream-telling, based on "the psychic trivia of a
boring character," as objectionable and smacking of
"self-engrossed narcissism."

405.   Sublette, Walter. "To the World of the Rusty Dead."
        Oui, May 1974, pp. 31-2. -
        Reluctantly emerging from this intense, compell-
ing, and brilliant "experience of flesh and mind,"
Sublette praises its successful fusion of sex, psychological conflict, and attraction of death and Allert's
mesmerizing power over us. He finds that Hawkes is
a "superb writer who compels us to sympathetic understanding by opening rusty doors that lesser writers
don't even know exist," as he maintains that Allert
has the ability to allow us to share his sexual encounters.

406.   Thompson, R. J. Review of Death, Sleep & the Trav-
        eler. Best Sellers 34 (May 15, 1974): 95-6. +
        Hawkes has "one of the most commanding imagi-
nations in modern fiction," which displays itself in a
powerful poetic style that allows us to "see each scene
as if it were happening on the slopes of Olympus for
all time." He invents new myths and translates the
adventures of a Mary Poppins or Bob and Alice and
Ted and Carol to lunar landscapes. In the present
work he appears to confront Allert and us with "epis-
temological problems of seeing and dreaming and know-
ing." In answer to protesting superrealists, his meta-
fiction is most true to life when least clear.

407.   Todd, Richard S.   "Getting Real, ... Puzzlement and
        Terror." Atlantic Monthly, May 1974, p. 130;
        excerpted in Contemporary Literary Criticism,
        pp. 216-7 (No. 586).   -
        Though unclear about this "pompous" novel's
events and their significance, enjoys the graceful style
and "luminous scenes" and talks of Allert's inner battle as one between the forces of clarity and those of
murk.   Thinks that great praise of Hawkes is unjusti-
fied by his "narrow, gamelike, self-protective work."

408.   Truehart, Charles.   "The Big Sleep and A to Z."
        Greensboro (North Carolina) Daily News, April
        28, 1974, p. D-3.   +
        Feels that even more than parody Hawkes intends
by his tongue-in-cheek stance in this novel to present
Allert as an example of the "20th-century picaresque
hero," a type perfected by John Barth.   Moreover,
judges that as a collection of short scenes written not
for the story but for the characters, most of whom
suffer from a "debilitating anomie," it is successful.

409.   V., J.   "Les Cauchemars familiers de John Hawkes."
        Tribune de Genève, February 28, 1975, p. 37.   -
        Considers that Hawkes's novels present to us
scenes which are nightmarish but are close to the reality of everyday happenings.   Provides a quick insight into Allert's personality while outlining the action of the book.

410.   Weinberg, Helen.   "Death, Sleep and the Traveler."
        Cleveland Plain Dealer, May 5, 1974, p. 5G.   +
        Declares that "America's best surrealist novelist"
has perfected his images greatly since The Cannibal
and in this work "combines a profound sense of the
mythic with a clean narrative and a central figure of
engaging and curious particularity."   Discusses Allert's attributes, noting the dependence of the story
on his dreams and memories.   Comments also on the
haunting sense of ambiguous alternatives in the novel
and infers from its inclusion of men different from
Allert that "Everyman is no simple creature with a
discoverable true way."   States, finally, Hawkes's success in accomplishing the "ultimate goal of surrealistic literature by making dream reality."

411.   Williams, Carol.   " 'Death, Sleep, etc.'." Raleigh

News & Observer, May 19, 1974, sec. 4, p. 7.
-
   Less violent than The Blood Oranges and more
successful in its symmetry of threes than with the two
couples of this previous work, nonetheless, the novel's
bizarre nature appears in the detached characters and
style. "It could have stood more work," but since
Hawkes appears to be gaining in his "working out,
book by book, a style and method," I'll be awaiting
his next novel.

412.   Wood, Michael. "O Tempora! O Moors!" New
          York Review of Books, August 8, 1974, pp. 40-1;
          excerpted in Contemporary Literary Criticism,
          p. 219   (No. 586).   *
       Analyzes Allert, "a curiously composed narrator
of his own alarming dreams," whose story suggests
that "placid normality is riddled with the raw material of madness." Though discovering triviality at the
heart of the book, regards the glittering style as "the
perfect vehicle for Hawkes's fastidiously upsetting effects." Concludes, however, that this work and The
Blood Oranges lack substance and "have the air of
dazzling exercises performed on the edge of nothing."

SEE ALSO: Nos. 417, 420, 422, 433, 445.

                         Travesty

413.   Allen, Bruce. "The Equal Halves of Good and Evil."
          Boston Sunday Globe, April 25, 1976, p. 80.   -
       "What happens to the artist determined to liberate
himself from all irrelevant constraints; to the ordinary man bent on breaking through beyond ordinari-
ness," is the pattern that arises from this and Hawkes's
other two latest novels. Travesty is a cunningly-de-
signed work, whose numerous implications are almost
anti-human and whose central character is the travesty, as he carries out his plan to bring about "artistic
construction" through "made death." A work of "marvelous and seductive virtuosity," and probably the
first of Hawkes's novels with its surface meanings so
cleverly, economically, and elegantly presented, it is
the best introduction to the work of a writer who may
be appreciated fully only by generations to come.

414.   Bruni, Thomas G.   Review of Travesty.   Lehigh Val-
          ley Labor Herald (Allentown, Pa.), April 9, 1976,
          p. 6.
          "A typical John Hawkes novel, a brief but tensely
       terrifying tour de force" with "richly insinuating iron-
       ies and meticulous delineation of the absurd." Pos-
       sibly Hawkes is "America's most polished stylist."

415.   [Brussat, Frederic A.]   "Death-ridden Novels."   Cul-
          tural Information Service 7 (April 1976): 15.   -
          Another of Hawkes's post-Modern novels which
       deal with what he calls "the conflict between sexual
       or life possibilities and drives toward destruction and
       death," this fabulation shows the novelist's interest in
       creating shocking and mysterious fictional landscapes
       and his preoccupation with language.   Indeed, "Hawkes
       wants us to float on the cloud of language and affirm
       with him imagination as a stay against death."

416.   Duke, Maurice.   "Publishing Activity Stepped Up."
          Richmond Times-Dispatch, April 25, 1976, p. G5.
          Not for the casual reader but a fascinating book
       for those who "have a firm grasp of the literary tra-
       ditions of the 20th century."

417.   Frank, Sheldon.   "John Hawkes' Imitation Travesty."
          Chicago Daily News, March 20, 1976, p. 11.   +
          Though hailed for almost thirty years by many
       critics as "our foremost experimental novelist," John
       Hawkes has produced with Travesty "a dead and empty
       book."   Unlike his earlier novels, this recent work,
       like The Blood Oranges and Death, Sleep & the Trav-
       eler, lacks complexity and demonstrates that its "sin-
       ister tone" and "ominous air" are just "mysterioso
       effects, atmospherics."   It is a ridiculous novel and
       a travesty in the sense that it is "an empty, foolish
       imitation of a serious novel."

418.   Freedman, James O.   "It's Worth the Striving."
          Philadelphia Bulletin, April 18, 1976, sec. 5,
          p. 16.
          Never easy to comprehend, Hawkes's novels, in-
       cluding the latest, on the other hand, offer a vision
       of life and death that is worth our effort to try to un-
       derstand.

419.   Gilboy, J. Thomas.   Review of Travesty.   Best

Seller 36 (June 1976): 69. o
Numerous unanswered questions still fill my mind
concerning this novel. However, I have no doubt that
the work has "a fitness of metaphor, an urgent and
tough poetic use of sound, and a masterful use of auto-
mobile symbolism" which make it "worthy of Hawkes's
reputation. "

420.   Goldhammer, Alan.   "A Short Journey into Death and
       Human Psyche. "   Ithaca Journal, March 13, 1976,
       p. 3I.   +
       Offers an explanation of the meaning of this novel
in the light of Hawkes's previous two novels, all three
being considered a triad "concerned with sex, myth,
death and the psyche. " Indicates the constants in the
three works (middle-aged narrator, sexual relationships ended by death, nightmare atmosphere) and the
crucial implications of Death, Sleep & the Traveler
for Travesty. Wonders, in conclusion, about Hawkes's
future acceptance by the general readership but urges
potential readers to make the effort to sample the
work of "one of the master craftsman [sic] of free
form fiction. "

421.   Granetz, Marc.   "Design in Debris. "   Harvard Inde-
       pendent, April 15-21, 1976, p. 14.   +
       Whereas Hawkes's early works lacked a "sense of
unified experience, " the three latest novels delicately
balance "tale and telling. " This new novel, portraying
a world of "exquisite tension, " includes Hawkes's own
plea for a more imaginative public and mocks, among
other things, our contemporary lives. Travesty, in
which "beauty is fully informed by truth, " is a "vision
of the co-mingling of death, sex, and artistic myth, "
signaling Hawkes's attainment of writing maturity.

422.   Hayes, Brian.   "Fun Games and the Sexual Elite. "
       Baltimore Sun, April 25, 1976, p. D-7.   +
       Voicing his disappointment in Hawkes's trilogy,
which is concluded by Travesty, Hayes notes the similarities among the narrators of the three novels and
among the themes ("the meaning of personal loss, " a
"rigid and self-righteous version of marital liberality, "
and the "existence of a sexual elite"). He disparages
the novelist's "mystical vision of sex, " while acknowl-
edging a literary precedence in the works of D. H.
Lawrence, Henry Miller, and Thomas Wolfe. More-

over, Hayes wonders what Hawkes is attempting to
do with these novels, if, as is possible, he is not
serious in treating his themes.

423. Hipkiss, R. A. Review of Travesty. Long Beach
       Press-Telegram, April 14, 1976, p. P-6; also
       in Long Beach Independent, April 15, 1976, p.
       Z-1. +
       Although it requires a bit of study for understand-
       ing, this novel presents an intriguing "ironic portrait
       of the would-be suicide-murderer who thinks he has
       made an existential choice." While in style the work
       is reminiscent of Robbe-Grillet's works and in delin-
       eation of the monologist it recalls Browning's Duke of
       Ferrara and Dostoevsky's Raskolnikov, it is, above
       all, a mockery of the existentialistic writings of such
       authors as Camus, Hemingway, and Sartre.

424. Isle, Walter. "Hawkes' New Novel Is Simpler--Or Is
       It?" Houston Chronicle, April 25, 1976, Zest
       Magazine section, p. 16. +
       The fiction of John Hawkes, the first to be termed
       "anti-realistic," has always been difficult, although re-
       cent novels show an effort to simplify. The novel in
       hand, "a short simple narrative" on the surface, but
       growing more complex with closer readings, presents
       a study of the relationship of love and death to imagi-
       nation, in which the "imagination of disaster" plays a
       major part. For the sake of discovering true compas-
       sion we are made to endure "the absurdity and vio-
       lence of the action" and a continuous monologue by a
       ruthless narrator with an irritating voice. Yet we
       are drawn to the narrative by the novel's "heightened
       dramatic situation," powerful language, and our own
       fascination with the imagined violent accident.

425. Kizilos, A. P. "Where the Action Is: the Imagina-
       tion." Minneapolis Tribune, April 18, 1976, p.
       12D. +
       This newest "luminous deterioration" of Hawkes
       lacks his normal poetic achievement but has his char-
       acteristic imaginative power. Throughout the book,
       the reader is cognizant of the narrator's madness de-
       spite his brilliant, dispassionate language and feels
       a tension sustained by his own hope that the accident
       will not occur. Assuredly, an experimental fiction,
       quite like Camus' The Fall in structure, this novel

"will challenge if not convince the reader who values
philosophic reflection and poetic irony. "

426.   Knapp, John V.   "Deadly Trip to Purity. " Chicago
       Sun-Times, March 21, 1976, Book Week section,
       p. 9.   +
       Summarizing the action of this "bleak" novel, in-
fluenced by Camus' The Fall, Knapp suggests that its
real subject "concerns the possibility of aesthetic value and order in a post-modern, post-industrial world"
and describes the narrator's intentions in carrying out
his murderous plan. He considers this work to be a
"superb aesthetic experience" by the "most difficult of
the great American novelists" and also one of the
most rewarding.

427.   LeClair, Thomas (Edmund).   Review of Travesty.
       New Republic, May 8, 1976, pp. 26-7.   +
       LeClair believes that this novel is a minor work
but a "remarkable and welcome coda" to Hawkes's major novels.   He asserts that in completing Hawkes's
trilogy it reduces the materials of the other two novels
"into a parodic fable of failed eroticism. " He sees
the book, too, as an examination of some of Hawkes's
impulses as a writer, an examination which parodies
Anthony Alvarez's so-called "art of suicide" but also
leads the novelist to exaggerate some of his normal
fictional elements in a move towards self-revelation.
While LeClair insists that the novel lacks some of
Hawkes's best techniques, he refers to the narrator as
a hypnotic, though absurd, madman and to Hawkes's
continual use of a "context of absence" as resulting in
"an extraordinary focusing of attention. "

428.   McCabe, Carol.   "As Serious As a Sheet of Flame. "
       Providence Sunday Journal, April 25, 1976, Arts
       and Travel section, p. H-35.   +
       Assesses Hawkes as a writer who demands reader
participation in the creation of his novels, is as "serious as a sheet of flame, " and "is writing a new chapter in American literature. " Following a short sketch
of the characters and story of the book, notes the novelist's ability to write "more disturbingly erotic passages" than anyone else.

429.   McLaughlin, Lissa.   "Eros As First-Person Narra-
       tor. " Brown Daily Herald, May 14, 1976, Fresh

Fruit section, p. 10. +
This is Hawkes's " 'travesty' of pornographic fiction in both a structural and thematic sense," where
the "repeated climaxes of the traditional erotic plot"
are parodied, and the reader's sensations and expec-
tations manipulated. It is, as well, a "profound piece
of fiction," which investigates the close relationship
of sex and death and portrays life as void of innocence and borne out of "the imagination's own dark
and poetic plans." Despite his use of voyeuristic preoccupations indicative of traditional sexist premises
in this book, Hawkes is "a breathtaking stylist" and
has transformed the erotic novel into an exposition of
"Eros' darker and more murderous veins."

430.   Moss, Robert F. Review of Travesty. Saturday Re-
            view, March 20, 1976, p. 25. o
        Lacking the typical Hawkesian "vicious surreal-
ism" and "stylistic density" of past novels, the work
is very clear but contains a landscape "too airless
to sustain life" and so many overtones from other literary models as to "leave little room for a personal
voice."

431.   Nicol, Charles. "Imaginary Death." National Review,
            April 30, 1976, p. 461. +
        Long "one of our most admirable writers,"
Hawkes writes novels whose situations, neither quite
real nor overtly fantastic, "compel us to recognize
that we harbor their equivalents within ourselves."
His works are usually satisfying and rich with details
that only on occasion seem mannered. Yet, this new
novel, while splendid at times, is, on a whole, disappointing because it is actually a "single sustained
moment, and really does not have the stamina of a
novel." Moreover, despite the advertising about a
trilogy, this book is not related to the previous two.
Newcomers to Hawkes, pick another with which to be-
gin.

432.   Olson, Clarence E. "Speeding toward Silence." St.
            Louis Post-Dispatch, March 28, 1976, p. 4-F.
            o
        Largely delves into the psyche of Hawkes's nar-
rator, "a bored sensualist toying with a powerful undercurrent of sadomasochism." Praises the novel as
a "carefully honed nightmare" and likens it to "a

highly polished bit of ebony--beautiful but opaque,
and therefore terrifying. "

433.   Ottenberg, Eve. "Pick a Careening Chiller..." Phil-
       adelphia Inquirer, March 14, 1976, p. 10-E.   -
       Wholly comprised of the narrator's monologue,
this novel displays a "wonderfully tight style," which
mingles "death, love and indifference ... perfectly,
chillingly. " Features common to all three books in
the trilogy are the theme of "the connection between
death and nonmonogamous sexuality" and the mixture
of past, present, and future.   In Travesty the latter
trait especially leads to a "deep, stream-of-con-
sciousness intimacy with one character's inner life. "
Hawkes is "one of the best now writing. "

434.   Pendleton, Dennis. Review of Travesty.   Library
       Journal 101 (March 15, 1976):   834.
       "This fascinating horror story is quintessential
Hawkes, without the overwriting and difficulty he has
been accused of....   Hawkes's skill makes his [the
narrator's] madness plausible and compelling. "

435.   Perkins, Michael. "The Gross & the Grotesque. "
       Screw, April 12, 1976, p. 21.   +
       "Hawkes is a supremely gifted stylist who brings
to the erotic novel the ability to arouse, to amuse,
and to terrify. " This brilliant, brief work, a monologue by a "poetic, philosophical, and obsessively
lucid" narrator, shows Hawkes's awareness of the
"intimate connection between eroticism and death" and
is "Baudelairean in its claustrophobic evocation of the
sickly flowers of eros and death. "

436.   Plummer, William. Review of Travesty.   Bookletter
       2 (March 15, 1976):   14-5.   -
       For the most part Plummer analyzes the narra-
tor's intentions and accomplishments in this "paean
to the imagination. " Likening the work with its untra-
ditional style to a "necklace with pearls of different
hues strung on the most tenuous of threads," he
warns the reader that he may be pleased with Hawkes's
rhetoric yet "unsettled by the thought that premedi-
tated murder and suicide may be the highest act of
the imagination. "

436a. Pocalyko, Michael.   "Hawkes Symposium Set for

Weekend. " Muhlenberg Weekly (Allentown, Pa.),
April 8, 1976, pp. 7-8. +
Travesty, "beautiful and disturbing," is a "non-
restrained, poetic, and sentiently powerful piece of
erotic-lyric fiction. " It is a "cruel and multitonal
monologue" by a narrator who is motivated possibly
to carry out his murderous plans by the sexual multi-
plicities of himself and his family, who repeatedly insists upon his "poetic vision," and who ultimately reveals to the attentive reader an episode from his past
that is disclosed as a haunting travesty.

437.   Pochoda, Elizabeth. "Books." Glamour, July 1976,
          pp. 61-2. [61] -
        This is the last volume of a trilogy begun with
The Blood Oranges, in which "fantasy and eroticism
are put on trial to see where they lead to when no one
is allowed to blink or turn away. " Travesty's horror
is quiet but convincing and will prompt many to read
Hawkes's fine, earlier novels.

438.   Review of Travesty. Booklist 72 (March 1, 1976):
          959.
        Hawkes charges the reader to decide if the nov-
el's action represents "horrible reality" or absurdity
and then "to sweat it out or play along."

439.   Review of Travesty. Chicago Tribune, March 28,
          1976, sec. 7, p. 2.
        This "deliberate and highly sophisticated" travesty
"of the work and death of Albert Camus" is both brilliant and unnerving.

440.   Review of Travesty. Kirkus Reviews 44 (January 1,
          1976): 24-5. o
        "Despite the arousing insets ... the story evolves
somewhat too simplistically to even suggest the talents
of this foremost practitioner of avant-garde fiction.
It all seems to be taking place in an overconceptual-
ized vacuum. "

441.   Review of Travesty. New Yorker, April 19, 1976,
          p. 134. o
        A "hollow and coolly elegant novel," in which the
themes are the same as the other two novels of the
trilogy but which does not offer the reader anything
beyond the closed door of understanding except more

closed doors: "an endless succession of ornately
painted panels."

442.   Review of Travesty. Publishers Weekly 209 (Febru-
       ary 16, 1976): 80. o
       Meant to provide a libertine's rumination on "ex-
istential discontents," this work, on the contrary, has
little passion or genuine angst, offering instead an
"icy, self-satisfied monologue" and a finale which is
"a gesture of self-destruction neither dramatic nor
meaningful to anyone except the crazed driver."

443.   Sauls, Roger. "Travesty Completes Trilogy." Char-
       lotte Observer, March 14, 1976, p. 10C.   -
       Along with indicating the story of the novel, Sauls
interprets the narrator's outlook on his intended deed,
"his ultimate sensual act." He judges this book of
"tensile strength" to be akin to a meditation, "a fine
mechanism of thought tuned to the mind's shadow
side."

444.   Simon, Jeff. "Thriving on 'Design, Debris'." Buf-
       falo Evening News, April 3, 1976, p. C12.   -
       Grotesque, hugely powerful, as sharp as a black
diamond and "as destructive and pure as an ice
storm," this is possibly Hawkes's most extraordinary
novel. Its most glorious feature is its poetic language, bearing out the truth that this novelist has
"one of the most precisely lyrical and coldly affect-
ing prose styles in the English language."

445.   Tanner, Tony. Review of Travesty. New York
       Times Book Review, March 28, 1976, pp. 23-4.
       *
       Though beginning with a summary of Travesty,
Tanner attempts, thereafter, to explain why "Hawkes
is perhaps the most 'disturbing' contemporary American writer." He indicates important connections
among the novels of the trilogy and expresses the
opinion that Cyril's view of the "failed Illyria" in The
Blood Oranges arises in a sinisterly perverted form
in each of the next two novels, where both narrators
are psychopaths. Moreover, he suggests that even
the title, Travesty, points to the psychopathic derangement of the narrator in this book, since such
derangement "is a travesty of human reason." Yet
Tanner names a pleasurable derangement not the

perversions in the latest novel but the lack of any
stable guide posts to the way in which it should be
read.   His final declaration praises Hawkes as "one
of the very best living American writers" and Travesty as "one of his [Hawkes's] most remarkable fictions."

446.   Trueheart, Charles.   "Captive Audience."   Greens-
         boro (North Carolina) Daily News, March 21,
         1976, p. B-3.   +
       Elucidates the action of the novel and reflects up-
on the narrator's "detached, passionless" frame of
mind, which gives this fantasy a distinct air of reality.   Observes that suspense is here added to dramatic power, Hawkes's forte.

447.   Vandenberg, Laura L.   "Madman Speeds to Planned
         Crash."   Atlanta Constitution, April 25, 1976, p.
         10C.   -
       Travesty is "a landmark in modern literature's
attempts to create an idiosyncratic mythology of madness."   Written by one of America's finest living
writers, it is united with the two prior novels in its
"depiction of the mythological battle between sex and
death" within the mind of the narrator and is over-
whelming in the "magnitude and artistry of his
[Hawkes's] communicated vision."   Especially brilliant is "the construction of the sense of speed through
the deliberate and imperturbable meanderings of a
madman's monologue."

448.   Weinberg, Helen.   "Begone, John Hawkes, with Your
         Pessimism."   Cleveland Plain Dealer, March 21,
         1976, sec. 5, p. 9.   +
       Admitting failure to find any meaning in the nar-
rator's voyage of death, Weinberg assesses this novel,
not quite termed a disaster, to be an unsuccessful
aesthetic experiment.   She requests for the work a
story "to provide a moral context for the event described," although she concludes with a tongue-in-
cheek admission that perhaps her optimistic Bicenten-
nial attitude is responsible for her rejection of the
pessimism found in the book.

B. SHORT FICTION

Lunar Landscapes

449. Bishop, Tom. Review of Lunar Landscapes. Satur-
        day Review, August 9, 1969, p. 31. +
        "A valuable sampler of Hawkes's fiction," this
collection shows the novelist's concern solely with the
private anguish of his charactrs and their mythic rep-
resentation, as best exemplified in Charivari.   A
flair for the grotesque appears especially in The Owl.
But Hawkes's prose, though beautiful, ominously reveals "the twilight of the soul" and relates too little
to life.   Also, these stories exhibit an indulgence in
exoticism and, while generally proving that "John
Hawkes is one of the finer stylists writing in English
today," do not "mark him as one of the more compelling voices in current American fiction. "

450. Brady, Charles A. "Chilling Tales for Hot Days Of-
        fered in Three Volumes. " Buffalo Evening News,
        July 5, 1969, p. B-12.
        Thinks that "Death of an Airman" best achieves
Hawkes's aim of creating subtle terror but states that
the three novellas "have not worn well. "

451. Broberg, Jan. "Tre Amerikaner" [Three Americans].
        Ostersunds Posten (Sweden), August 30, 1969, p.
        2. o
        Typical of Hawkes's works, these stories are
nearly hallucinatory and have a gothic quality akin to
Walpole's and a style which effectively creates various moods.   However, the novellas are least original,
although the "Death of an Airman" has admirable concentration ("har en beundransvärd koncentration").

452. F. , W. ". . . While Hawkes Still Waits. " Kansas
        City Star, June 1, 1969, p. 3D.   -
        Hawkes is a prime example of the writer "who
find[s] life a horror and approach[es] physical experience as a fearsome ordeal," especially in writing of
"relationships with wives and children. "   Though
pleasurable to but a small group of readers, Hawkes's
cryptic fictions, reminiscent of Gertrude Stein's works,
doubtlessly have more meaning than is apparent on
the surface.

453.   Fowles, Jib. "Depthless Scenes." New Leader, May
        12, 1969, pp. 26-8. *
        "Convenient steppingstones for the reader not yet
        familiar with Hawkes," these stories are landscapes
        which are " 'lunar' in the sense that they stand on the
        very periphery of our cognizance." They demonstrate
        the novelist's avoidance of the hackneyed, tendency to-
        wards obscurity, and preference for unusual structure.
        Unfortunately, all of Hawkes's works bear a relent-
        less uniformity of tone and a sameness among the
        characters, but the intensely-written scenes mark his
        genius, and his language is stunning. Aided by ap-
        peals to the senses, many scenes from this collection
        "linger fiendishly in the memory."

454.   Green, James L(ee).   Review of Lunar Landscapes.
        Studies in Short Fiction 7 (Fall 1970): 676-8. *
        Focuses on the theme and substance of each work
        in the collection, noting Hawkes's feeling that "man is
        involved in deadly, self-perpetuating cycles of destruc-
        tion" and the novelist's aim to illuminate this "night-
        mare of human existence." Describes how each piece
        revolves around the idea that "life is a process of
        death," and devotes most space to Charivari, "a sa-
        tiric epithalamium to modern marriage," The Owl,
        portraying the growth of "life-denying traditions and
        rituals of death," and The Goose on the Grave, in
        which the natural part of man appears to survive "on
        the grave of the world."

455.   Heath, William (Ralph). Review of Lunar Landscapes.
        Kenyon Review 32 (1970/1): 186-90. *
        After explaining the meaning of the title and par-
        tially quoting Hawkes's explanation to New Directions
        in 1961 of his experimental intent in these stories,
        notes the novelist's stated emphasis on style. Points
        out Hawkes's frequent failure to attain his stylistic
        aim, although admitting the great contribution these
        pieces made towards developing his "poetic richness
        and psychic liberation." In fact, sees in the three
        novellas included in the collection "an interesting
        range of verbal accomplishment and psychological
        realization." Especially applauds the possibility of
        scholarly criticism of Hawkes's corpus with this pub-
        lication.

456.   Jordan, Clive. "Death's Emblems." New Statesman,

May 1, 1970, p. 634.   -
Written in true Gothic tradition and enlivened by
Hawkes's "ability to embody physical detail perfectly
in language," these stories display something like love
surviving in "an atmosphere of moral deadness."
Charivari especially shows Hawkes's unusual use of
time and suspense, while The Owl offers a "glimpse
of the mental processes of the Inquisition."

457.   Louik, Oscar.   "Book of Hawkes' Short Fiction Is
       Greeted Warmly."   Minneapolis Tribune, June 22,
       1969, p. 8E.   o
       Calls Hawkes "a supreme stylist," pointing out,
among other features, the novelist's unexcelled sentence rhythms.   Employing some of the stories as examples, demonstrates briefly how "Hawkes is more
trenchant than Kafka" and uses allegory effectively.

458.   Mahon, Derek.   "Games and Cases."   Listener, May
       21, 1970, p. 693.   -
       This collection of stories, the most impressive of
which is "The Nearest Cemetery," is "distinguished
by a fine professionalism that narrowly avoids being
merely slick."   Sometimes, too, as in Charivari,
"the apparently random accretion of casual data seems
too computerised to be likeable."

459.   Minor, William.   "Shelter without Comfort, from
       John Hawkes."   Milwaukee Journal, June 1, 1969,
       part 5, p. 4.   -
       Holding some of Hawkes's works to be over-
wrought, nonetheless agrees that the novelist is justly
admired for his imagination.   Chooses examples from
the novellas to demonstrate that Hawkes's characters
"are what surrounds them" and suggests that these
surroundings, as eerie and outlandish as the moon,
may not be dissimilar to our own land or homes.

460.   Moon, Eric.   Review of Lunar Landscapes.   Library
       Journal 94 (June 15, 1969): 2486.   o
       John Hawkes, "least-known, least-read writer of
quality on the American fiction scene," rightly has
gained a reputation for his obscurity and surrealism
because of his unique style and language.   His potential for writing The Lime Twig, "one of the best novels of the last decade," is visibly seen in the brilliant work, The Owl.

461.   Nye, Robert. "Gossip and Stories." Manchester
        Guardian, May 7, 1970, p. 9.
            Lunar Landscapes collects a number of Hawkes's
        finest fictions and "is characterised by the restless-
        ness of its imagination and the extreme precision of
        its prose style."

462.   Review of Lunar Landscapes. Choice 6 (November
        1969): 1222.
            A tedious work, which "appears to have been writ-
        ten for classroom exercises."

463.   Review of Lunar Landscapes. Publishers Weekly 195
        (January 27, 1969): 90. o
            As creator of "highly personal and richly imagina-
        tive landscape[s]" and an atmosphere of fantasy some-
        times hinting at and at other times powerfully evoking
        reality, Hawkes will be appreciated by those "who tune
        in to his strange world." Of special interest in this
        collection is the extraordinary novella, Charivari.

464.   Review of Lunar Landscapes. Virginia Quarterly Re-
        view 45 (Autumn 1969): cxxviii; excerpted in Con-
        temporary Literary Criticism, p. 213 (No. 586).
        o
            "No writer in America is more scrupulous, or
        ruthless, than Hawkes, and none has given us fictions
        of greater imaginative purity and power." Found in
        this collection, The Owl and The Goose on the Grave
        are works of precise, beautiful language, uncanny ter-
        ror, and intense vision.

465.   Rowes, Barbara. "John Hawkes: Wrong Genre."
        Washington Post, October 1, 1969, p. B-9.   -
            Hawkes's surrealistic fiction concerns the "funda-
        mental divisions wihin man's own nature," placing a
        greater emphasis on absurdity than even his predeces-
        sors Barnes or Céline. Unfortunately, these nine
        short stories are "too small in scope to reflect
        Hawkes's universe," which is based on opposition,
        and are overburdened by the metaphorical language,
        which is very effective in the novels.

466.   Scholes, Robert. Review of Lunar Landscapes. New
        York Times Book Review, July 13, 1969, pp. 4-
        5, 32.   *
            Recommending this volume as an excellent intro-

duction to Hawkes's work, states that the novelist is
trying to expose "the depths of our own planet and
its inhabitants," illuminated by the often beauteous
light of his "nocturnal imagination." Finds Charivari
to be "a brilliant piece of surrealistic satire," which
captures the sense of Hawkes's "astonishing and so
aggressively avant-garde" beginnings. Deems The
Owl to be equally extraordinary with its demonstration
of Hawkes's later, more unified, vision as it tackles
the subject of "the immense King's evil of history."

467.   Schott, Webster. "Nightmare World of John Hawkes."
        Life [Regional edition], September 19, 1969, p.
        R-[4], between pp. 22 and 23.   +
        Still virtually unlike any other American novelist
        since his first novel twenty years ago, Hawkes can be
        called "the Gothic sorcerer of modern American let-
        ters." By combining imagination, occult literary tech-
        niques such as "distortion, hallucination [and] necro-
        philic metaphor," and cold, oracular, but glowing,
        language, he continues to create "a new anti-real
        world that makes a black romance of the fast world
        we live in." Charivari, The Owl, The Goose on the
        Grave and the other works in this collection lack the
        maturity of Hawkes's later novels but gloriously pres-
        ent, nevertheless, his unparalleled imaginary worlds.

468.   Sheats, Audrey. "Hawkes: A Sense of Strangeness."
        Los Angeles Times, June 8, 1969, Calendar sec-
        tion, p. 51.   +
        The unique, dispassionate prose style of John
        Hawkes is clear and strong with a precision that
        makes ordinary happenings seem grotesque. These
        stories, peopled also with grotesque characters and
        delineated in rather a formless, fragmented manner,
        proclaim that "reality is incomprehensible." Yet
        such works have little appeal to the reader looking
        for suspenseful action and fully-formed characters.

469.   "Some That Survived." Times Literary Supplement,
        July 2, 1970, p. 701.
        Names Hawkes "a deliberate experimenter,"
        whose stories demonstrate that "human society ... is
        dark and cruel and full of monsters as any moon."

470.   Spachs, Barry. "Master Stylist of Fantasy." Bos-
        ton Sunday Globe, August 17, 1969, p. 20-A.   -

"A generously inventive writer" and "one of the master-stylists of our time," Hawkes, employing a prose described by the young novelist, Jerome Charyn, as "poetic troubled language under grave pressure, amid chaos and terror," expresses "our deepest fears and fantasies, anticipations and desires," but sometimes causes tedium with his unusual language and viewpoint. These stories are "ceremonies of experience," the most powerful of which is The Owl.

471. Thornton, Eugenia. "Short Gems." Cleveland Plain Dealer, June 29, 1969, p. 7F.
These stories of "icy brilliance" by one of our best writers indicate the novelist's serene outlook on turbulence, "which draws the truth out of violent happenings."

472. Wain, John. "The Very Thing." New York Review of Books, February 26, 1970, pp. 35-8. [36-7]

It is depressing to see stories by such a gifted writer that are nearly unreadable. They are overwritten, lack development, and are "determinedly planted in a no-man's land between the observed and the imagined that misses the cogency of either."

SEE ALSO: No. 317, reviews of Charivari, The Goose on the Grave, and The Owl.

Other Stories

473. "American Review Is Still Unique." Painesville Telegraphic, February 17, 1973, p. 2.
Says of "The Universal Fears" that it "provides a glimpse of a male teacher's emotional courage after a brutal attack by delinquent girls."

474. "In Print." Los Angeles Magazine 18 (March 1973): 55.
Praises "The Universal Fears" as a "masterfully understated horror piece."

475. Kohler, Dayton. "Uneven Texture in the Stories Collected for New Directions 13." Louisville Courier-Journal, February 10, 1952, sec. 3, p. 11.
Refers fleetingly to "The Courier" as a "first-rate" story.

476. Koltz, Newton.   Review of American Review 16 and
        Fiction 3.   Village Voice, March 29, 1973, pp.
        25, 30.   [25]
        "The Universal Fears" is an example of Hawkes's
      "great talent for getting inside people who suck their
      own blood."

*477. Lothamer, Eileen.   Review of American Review 16.
        Long Beach Press-Telegram, March 21, 1973;
        also in Long Beach Independent, March 22, 1973,
        p. Z-4.
        Complete citation reads: "Hawkes' excellent study
      of the fifty-ish London teacher of 'The Universal
      Fears' sets the man, the girls, the fears so sharply
      that short commentary is futile.   Read it."

478. Thompson.   Francis J.   "Old and New."   Hopkins Re-
        view 5 (Spring 1952): 85-8.   [85]
        Concerning "The Courtier" of New Directions 13
      Thompson berates Hawkes for seeking "inspiration in
      the wake of remote depravity" [i. e. in totalitarianism]
      for this story and for the larger work from which it
      comes (The Goose on the Grave).   He charges the
      writer to become more formidable by introducing "im-
      agination into his fancy."

*479. Watkins, Edward.   "Seeing Stars."   Our Town (July
        6, 1973): 6
        Cites Hawkes's "The Universal Fears" in Ameri-
      can Review 16, a "harrowing portrait of a teacher who
      courts violence in a school for delinquent girls," as
      his favorite.

C. PLAYS

           Literary Reviews: The Innocent Party:
                    Four Short Plays

480. Burrows, Miles.   "Ceremonies of Experience."   New
        Statesman, November 10, 1967, pp. 644-5.   [644]
        These plays are "four humorous and menacing
      charades."   The Innocent Party is possibly a parody
      of Tennessee Williams, while The Questions, moving
      quickly and evenly, "denotes inspiration or profession-

alism" and is an "ironic tour de force."

481.   Davis, Douglas M.   "Blacker But Bleaker, the Latest
        from Some 'Black Humorists'."   National Observ-
        er, June 19, 1967, p. 19.
        Surreal and moody, but also thin and wispy, these
plays are "like fairy tales trying to be tragic."

482.   Dennis, Nigel. "Color It Orange."   New York Review
        of Books, July 13, 1967, pp. 6, 8.   #
        Following a description of The Innocent Party and
its characters, Dennis shouts out his confusion about
the meaning of the play.   Similarly, he expresses concern over the meanings of the other plays, with the
exception of The Questions, whose basic idea is seen
to be the same as that of Williams's Suddenly Last
Summer but treated in a far poorer manner.   Finally,
Dennis accuses both Mr. Blau and Hawkes of caring
nothing about the meaning of words and chides contemporary playwrights, in general, for solving writing
problems by using "meaningless words and stage 'bus-
iness'."

483.   "Improvisations and Rituals."   Times Literary Supple-
        ment, January 4, 1968, p. 15.   o
        Lacking the "sense of form or certainty of tone"
of their model, Tennessee Williams, the plays over-
emphasize dialogue and virtually cocoon small actions
in verbal preparation.

484.   "Notes etc. on books etc."   Carleton Miscellany 8
        (Fall 1967): 121.
        The reviewer voices his feeling in rather sarcas-
tic terms that Hawkes's plays are insignificant and
that Blau's comments on the plays are equally so.

485.   Oberbeck, S. K.   "Indianheads."   Newsweek, April 3,
        1967, pp. 93-4; excerpted in Modern American
        Literature, pp. 53-4 (No. 587).
        Declares that these plays, "more poetic than
Pinter and not a nightmare less scarifying than Iones-
co," have established Hawkes as "one of America's
most significant avant-garde dramatists."   Says, further, that, displaying the "sinuous surrealism of a
psychedelic poster," the plays disclose the "ugly inner
sanctums" of us all and portray the "painfully absurd
situations that plague human beings."

486.   R., J. W.   Review of The Innocent Party.   Prairie
           Schooner 42 (Fall 1968): 279.
           Attempting to create stage dialogue and to use
stage effects, Hawkes has really tried to produce theatrical pieces.   Perhaps The Questions will move audi-
ences like Pinter's plays.

487.   Review of The Innocent Party.   Antiquarian Bookman
           39 (May 15, 1967): 1955.
           "New writing, polished, readable and interesting,
not just avant."

488.   Review of The Innocent Party.   Booklist 63 (July 1,
           1967): 1126.
           Utilizes black comedy and Theater-of-the-Absurd
effects "to dramatize the impoverishment of body and
spirit that passes for existence in a society in which
false and empty morality pervades the fabric of its
social and sexual mores."

489.   Review of The Innocent Party.   Choice 4 (September
           1967): 698. o
           Finds these plays, too obviously influenced by ab-
surdist playwrights, to be "overloaded with symbolism" and frequently hindered by "dull, repetitious dialogue" and amateurishness.

490.   Review of The Innocent Party.   Kirkus 34 (August 1,
           1966): 820.
           Mainly quotes some of Herbert Blau's introductory
comments to The Innocent Party.

491.   Stiles, Patricia.   Review of The Innocent Party.   Li-
           brary Journal 92 (May 15, 1967): 1949. o
           Primarily of interest to those liking experimental
theater, these plays are all concerned with "the dis-
section of Innocence by several characters on a nearly
bare stage."

SEE ALSO: Nos. 164, 177.

                    Other Literary Reviews

492.   Heist, Jeremy W.   "The Harvard Advocate."   Har-
           vard Crimson, January 13, 1967, p. 2. o
           The Undertaker is a "surrealistic and occasionally

metaphysical father-son dialogue," which is often en-
igmatic. It contains prose that is highly mellifluous
and employs numerous salient images, perfectly
caught large and small effects, and "quiet, measured
tones" or "violent crescendoes," as the need indicates.

493.   Starb, August W.   "Five Plays and a Complaint."
        Southern Review n.s. 6 (July 1970):   853-6.
        [854] o
        Included in Plays for a New Theatre: Playbook
        2 is The Wax Museum, which will be shocking at
        times and will "play well" but will leave the audience
        wondering about its meaning.

                        Production Reviews

The Wax Museum

494.   Cund, John M.   "Two New Playwrights at Touraine."
        Christian Science Monitor, April 30, 1966, p. 7.
        o
        In reacting to the opening night production by the
        Theater Company of Boston, the reviewer admires
        Hawkes's inventiveness and the skill of the actors in
        their performance but laments the lack of substance
        and straining for effects in the play.   Cund's com-
        ments also apply to Rosalyn Drexler's The Investiga-
        tion, the other production of the evening.

495.   Dubkin, Pauline.   "TCB Finale: Of Witchhunts and
        Waxings."   Patriot Ledger, April 29, 1966, p.
        32.   -
        Hawkes's "stunning, sparkling little cameo" was
        performed by the Theater Company in an equally
        stunning and sparkling manner.   This is an "Albee-
        esque arabesque," in which the playwright tries to
        "both fuse and diffuse the barriers between illusion
        and reality" and deftly portrays "the mutability of two
        separate lives."

496.   Haskell, Molly.   "Two by Hawkes."   Village Voice,
        April 10, 1969, p. 44.   +
        "Like a department store, with its mythological
        multi-levels [and] its profusion of details," and featur-
        ing a wry curiosity which mixes detachment and a

somewhat grotesque affection, Hawkes's highly imagistic writing reveals itself far less in his plays. However, these Chelsea Theater productions of The Wax Museum and The Innocent Party are marvelous. The former displays more eroticism than seen anywhere else on the stage this year, and the latter, an unsettling, "witty and languid passivity" through funny, excellent performances.

497.   Hirsch, Samuel.   "New Form of Theater Not Really Plays at All." Boston Herald, May 2, 1966, p. 26. -
After attending the Theater Company of Boston's performances of The Investigation by Drexler and of The Wax Museum, pronounces both to be "adolescent daydreams of an abnormal deviant nature." Castigates the playwrights for continual use of words without artistic purpose, causing weariness in the reader, and for eliminating basic conflict and character revelation, promoting boredom. Detects embarrassment or boredom even in the actors.

498.   Maloney, Alta.   " 'Unrestricted Approach to Theater.' " Boston Traveler, May 2, 1966, p. 18-A.   -
Both The Wax Museum and The Investigation, performed by the Theater Company of Boston, indicate the playwrights' "knowledge of the human psyche with heavy emphasis on abnormal psychology," as well as skill in creating short dramatic works and in forming "a philosophic statement in remarkable terms." However, one wonders why these extraordinarily talented writers require self-assertion through obscenities rather than through acceptable language.

499.   Norton, Elliot.   "Two Unpleasant Dramas Done by Hub Theater Co." Boston Record American, May 5, 1966, p. 53. o
Praises the adroit staging and remarkable acting of the Theater Company's production of this "strikingly original, disturbing, disedifying" play. Doubts, nonetheless, that the play "will do anything for anyone with the possible exception of clinical psychologists."

500.   Safford, Edwin.   "Theater Company in Two New Plays." Providence Sunday Journal, May 1, 1966, p. W-17.   -

In this production Blythe Danner's acting is
"peachy," but the total effect of the play is comic.
Unfortunately, an amused reaction was probably not
the intention of the playwright.

501.   Stark, Larry. "Final New Plays at Theatre Co."
       Boston after Dark, May 4, 1966, p. 1.   o
       Misses Danner and Thornton gave excellent per-
formances, transforming a rather simple, predictable
story, based on the "eeriest of wax-museums" and
"on the passions that the 'chamber of horrors' taps
in us all," into something magical.

The Undertaker

502.   Kelly, Kevin. "A Pall of Despair in Theater Co.
       Twin Bill." Boston Globe, March 29, 1967, p.
       24.   -
       Feeling that there is little else to comment on,
Kelly dwells on the description of scenery and characters in this play.   He compliments Wheeler for directing well "the pauses in the conversation" and levels
criticism against Hector Elizondo for a "badly muffed"
portrayal of the father and against Larry Bryggman,
who, "not without reason," acted embarrassed to play
the son.

The Innocent Party (Theater Company of Boston Production)

503.   Hirsch, Samuel. " 'End of World' and 'Fun War'
       Lack Basic Craft and Purpose." Boston Herald
       Traveler, February 19, 1968, p. 20.
       Hawkes has a "pessimist's love for melancholy
metaphor" and takes too long a look at "the sterility
and the corruptive evil of poverty and wealth" in this
play.   His writing is cryptic, evasive and repetitious,
Wheeler's staging is often awkward, and the acting,
except that of Ms. Channing, is as one-dimensional as
the writing.

504.   Kelly, Kevin. "Paradise Complex." Boston Globe,
       February 16, 1968, p. 33.   +
       Considers Hawkes to be a "demonic dramatist of
considerable power," but also "of considerable confusion," who "writes with controlled ferocity" and "an

occasional spellbinding skill." Summarizes the plot
and provides an interpretation of the play, as well as
commending to the public Wheeler's directing and most
of the acting.

505. Norton, Elliot. "New 'Innocent Party' Drama Cruel,
     Cold-Blooded, Strong." Boston Record American,
     February 20, 1968, p. 33. +
     Norton accompanies his lengthy description of the
action of the play with compliments for the unusual
performances by Naomi Thornton and Susan Channing,
who played Phoebe and Jane, respectively. He sees
this "strong" play as a "cold-blooded study of four
people: two weak and defeated, two strong and cruel,
and of what happened when the weak ones pleaded and
the cruel ones clashed."

506. Reisman, Arnold. "Solid Gold Cataract." Patriot
     Ledger, February 16, 1968, p. 26. -
     In addition to a summary of the play's story of-
fers the opinion that while Hawkes's "bizarre satire"
is more profound and satiric than its companion play,
its structure is that of a rough draft. Observes jag-
ged moods and meanings and a "battle raging between
obscurity and ostentation" in the work. Nonetheless,
praises the cast's performance.

SEE ALSO: No. 496.

The Questions (Trinity Square and Stanford Little Theater
            Productions)

507. Atwood, Lois. "Trinity at Its Best: Adrian Hall Di-
     rects Contemporary, Dynamic Well-Acted Plays."
     Rhode Island Herald (Pawtucket), February 17,
     1967, p. 8. -
     Calls Hawkes's play a "mind-stretching exercise"
because of the variety of situations it could represent
and the number of characters "the man" could portray.
Especially admires Miss Payton-Wright's acting and
her apt rendition of the play's humorous lines.

508. Dusheck, George. "Young Girl Relives Papa's Nasty
     Act." San Francisco Examiner, January 14, 1966,
     p. B-3. o
     An excellently produced "interior monologue of

surprising although not irresistible interest," whose
theme is "the conflict between custom and feeling, between reality and poetry." Hawkes's good ear and
wit are evident. "Now, if he will just write a play
where something happens..."

509.   Heineman, Al(an). "The Questions: A Psychological
        Analysis." Stanford Daily, January 18, 1966, p.
        4.   +
        It is Heineman's belief that in this actionless play,
where "only talk, seldom leavened by highly-pitched
emotionalism" prevails, the end arrives with the Girl
steadfastly maintaining her "innocence." He hazards
guesses concerning the identity of the two characters
and underscores the ambiguity of the play, which he
feels is admirably preserved by the excellent acting.
Asserting further that the play does involve the audience intellectually, Heineman, on the other hand, concludes that its success depends on one's definition of
the function of the theater.

510.   Kelly, Kevin. "Brutal Brilliance Lights Double Bill."
        Boston Globe, February 17, 1967, p. 21.   -
        Unable to dispel this "dark ruminating nightmare"
from his mind, Kelly declares it to be a "psychoana-
lytic duologue exchange between a psychiatrist and his
patient" which is "fascinating, brilliantly worded and
flawlessly played."

511.   Leonard, Dave. "Stanford Dramas Create Interest."
        Palo Alto Times, January 14, 1966, p. 11.   -
        The Questions is a "strongly compelling drama,"
which, despite its unique approach to the idea behind
it, "cannot overcome its stasis" because of the over-
use of repetitive questioning. Though "more enjoyable
to think about than ... to sit through," the drama is
ably played and directed.

512.   Swan, Bradford. "2 Plays Staged at Trinity Square."
        Providence Journal, February 17, 1967, p. 8.   -
        Says that Hawkes is telling a highly literary short
story here and is not giving us a play. However,
praises the actors for their skill and artistry in imbu-
ing a sense of theater into this play.

PART V

BOOKS, SECTIONS OF BOOKS, AND NEWSPAPER AND JOURNAL ARTICLES ON HAWKES AND HIS WORKS

A. NOVELS

Charivari

513.   Green, James L(ee). "Nightmare and Fairy Tale in Hawkes' Charivari." Critique (Atlanta) 13, no. 1 (1971): 83-95.
    Green interprets this novelette, showing its fulfillment of Hawkes's early-stated emphasis on dream and nightmare in his writings and its similarity to an ordinary fairy tale--a fairy tale with an ironic ending, "undercutting the false security of dream, affirming, the reality of nightmare." Hawkes's fictional technique with its use of recurrent images and actions, related events, allusions, and symbols is explained. Marred only by the novelist's "occasional snickering intrusions," resulting from his attempts at extreme fictional detachment, in Green's estimation this work reveals "the enervation of the modern world" and focuses attention on the fundamental problems of human existence.

SEE ALSO: Nos. 570, 572, 578, 593, 603, 612-3, 617.

The Cannibal

514.   Dommergues, Pierre. Les Ecrivains américains d'aujourd'hui. Que sais-je?, no. 1168. Paris: Presses Universitaires de France, 1965, pp. 84-5.
    Inserts a few statements noting that the "lucid cruelty" of novels by William Burroughs also occurs in the works of John Hawkes and especially in The Cannibal.

143

515.   Fiedler, Leslie A.   Love and Death in the American
        Novel.   New York: Criterion Books, 1960, pp.
        455, 467-8.
        Just a few sentences are devoted to this work,
        but Fiedler makes his point that the novel is "incom-
        prehensibly neglected," since it presents surrealisti-
        cally a vision of post-World War II Europe "more ap-
        propriate to what we know than the inevitably ration-
        alist falsification of history."

516.   "First Novels among the Leading Spring Titles."
        Publishers Weekly 157 (January 14, 1950):   149.
        Mentions Albert Guerard's introduction to The
        Cannibal (see No. 517), "which New Directions will
        publish on March 1."   Adds the publisher's assess-
        ment of Hawkes's technique as "highly experimental."

517.   Guerard, Albert J.   Introduction to The Cannibal, by
        John Hawkes.   Norfolk, Conn.:   New Directions,
        1949, pp. vii-xiv; Introduction and Addendum to
        The Cannibal, by John Hawkes.   1st rev. Amer.
        ed., New York: New Directions, 1962, pp. ix-
        xx; excerpted in Modern American Literature,
        p. 49 (No. 587).
        Hawkes's former mentor attempts to promote un-
        derstanding and enjoyment of this work by removing
        "some of the peripheral difficulties and obstacles of
        strangeness."   He explains the plot and points out the
        distorted focus, lack of sympathy for characters, em-
        phasis on unimportant details, and elements of sur-
        realism.   Guerard feels that Hawkes has achieved not
        only a true picture of post-war Germany but also of
        our modern world.
        The later "Addendum" emphasizes the novel's
        long-livedness and its position as a "central work of
        art and vision."   Guerard also notes Hawkes's more
        recent movement towards a kind of realism but finds
        a continuation of the novelist's "imaginative strengths"
        and "vivifying distortion."

518.   Hassan, Ihab.   "The Dismemberment of Orpheus--
        Reflections on Modern Culture, Language, and
        Literature."   American Scholar 32 (Summer 1963):
        463-84.   [478]
        Devoting two paragraphs to Hawkes, Hassan first
        highlights the novelist's "grim humor of nightmares,"
        even including a quotation from Hawkes on the satiric

writer and his relationship to the novel. Next, he
remarks concerning The Cannibal that its style en-
ters the "twilight region between the rational and absurd."

519.　　　　　　. "The Existential Novel." Massachusetts
　　　　Review 3 (Summer 1962): 795-7. [797]
　　　　The barest mention of this novel is made as Hassan talks about books containing "distinct ironic ca-
tharsis."

520.　　　　　　. "The Novel of Outrage: A Minority Voice
　　　　in Postwar American Fiction." American Scholar
　　　　34 (Spring 1965): 239-53. [249-50]
　　　　Cannibalism appears to be a metaphor of outrage
in this book, in which the author presents to us a
totally blighted world where everything is permeated
by violence and nothing exists except the "atavistic
power of revenge." If Hawkes is a satirist, as he
proclaims himself to be, he aims his barbs at nature,
"which leers at the jocular antics of evil men."

521.　　　　　　. Radical Innocence: Studies in the Contem-
　　　　porary American Novel. Princeton: Princeton
　　　　University Press, 1961, p. 103.
　　　　Very briefly talks of this novel as an example of
a poetic work which is surreal and autistic but
through its form communicates the failure of communication of our time and touches upon the "inner
processes of the psyche: epiphany, myth, poetry,
drama."

522.　Hoffman, Frederick J. The Modern Novel in Amer-
　　　　ica, 1900-1950. Twentieth-Century Literature in
　　　　America. Chicago: Henry Regnery, 1951, pp.
　　　　180-1; The Modern Novel in America. 3rd rev.
　　　　ed. Chicago: Henry Regnery, 1963, pp. 198-9;
　　　　excerpted in Contemporary Literary Criticism,
　　　　p. 212 (No. 586).
　　　　This novel is a "surrealist evocation of European
despair," whose domination by various enormities sustain it as a "remote and terrible fantasy," lacking the
"profound significance of Kafka's fiction." It is an
example of how post-World War II novelists are attempting to break away from naturalism and, beyond
that, reaches a symbolic level of meaning about the
War, being neither a work of "raw documentation"

nor of "indifferent fantasy."

523.   Loukides, Paul.   "The Radical Vision."   Michigan
            Academician 5 (1973):   497-503.   [502-3]
          Examples are provided of how, like Heller's
       Catch-22, this work, representative of all of Hawkes's
       novels, transforms reality through language and, dis-
       regarding the traditional normative vision of reality,
       "leads us to the radical vision [of reality] distinct
       from both rationalistic and Christian orthodoxy."

524.   Reutlinger, D. P.   "The Cannibal: The Reality of
            Victim."   Critique (Atlanta) 6 (Fall 1963):   30-7.
          The Cannibal is Hawkes's "indictment of romantic
       politics and its victimization of a whole people."   De-
       picted in this work is a "community of victims," in
       which all of the members begin to feed upon one an-
       other in various ways.   Moreover, Hawkes's anti-
       realistic art objectifies and dehumanizes the victim-
       izers and victims so that the reader does not sympa-
       thetically identify with the victim but develops a deeper
       sympathy by intellectually apprehending the horrors.

525.   Vickery, Olga W.   "The Inferno of the Moderns."
            In The Shaken Realist; Essays in Modern Litera-
            ture in Honor of Frederick J. Hoffman, pp. 147-
            64.   [152-5] Edited by Melvin J. Friedman and
            John B. Vickery.   Baton Rouge: Louisiana State
            University Press, 1970; excerpted in Contempo-
            rary Literary Criticism, p. 213 (No. 586).
          In slightly more than a page Vickery describes
       how the images and situations of this work, especial-
       ly the grand image of Spitzen-on-the-Dein and the act
       of cannibalism, recall Dante's Inferno.   She credits
       the book's "realistic detail, psychological acumen, and
       controlled fantasy" to Hawkes's originality.

526.   Wegelin, Christof.   "The Cosmopolitanism of Power
            in American Fiction."   In International Federation
            for Modern Languages and Literatures, 12th Con-
            gress, Cambridge, 1972.   Expression, Communi-
            cation, and Experience in Literature and Language,
            pp. 220-2.   Edited by Ronald G. Popperwell.
            London: Modern Humanities Research Association,
            1973.   [221-2]
          Names this novel as the forerunner of some of
       the war novels of the 1960's which paint an absurd

picture of the world. Considers none of these later
novels, though, to be as vicious as Hawkes's in its
treatment of "the German post-war hell, " in which
war corrupts love "by turning the gestures of sexual
passion into weapons of destruction. "

SEE ALSO: Nos. 70, 81, 83, 531, 567-8, 570, 572, 577-8,
    581-4, 590-1, 593, 595, 597-8, 602-3, 609, 611,
    613, 615, 617, 619.

The Beetle Leg

527.   Frost, Lucy.   "The Drowning of American Adam:
           Hawkes' The Beetle Leg. " Critique (Atlanta) 14,
           no. 3 (1973): 63-74.
           Hawkes's present work utilizes all of the para-
    doxes which normally appear in his early novels to
    complete "a fiction vision which can be understood ...
    as a thoughtful and frightening illumination of contem-
    porary American culture. " Combining a distinctive
    "verbal landscape" with powerful imagery, Hawkes fash-
    ions this work on the pattern of the "biblical myth
    of Adam's Fall, together with the peculiarly American
    cultural myth of a new Eden" to depict the evolution
    of man to a highly technological state and man's sub-
    sequent devolution. As is usual in Hawkes's books,
    man is pictured as ultimately giving up his dreams
    and succumbing to apathy.

SEE ALSO: Nos. 76, 90, 531, 570, 572, 578, 581, 593,
    603, 609, 611, 613, 617.

The Goose on the Grave and The Owl

See Nos. 572, 578, 581, 590-1, 593, 597, 603, 609, 611,
    613, 617, 619.

The Lime Twig

528.   Boutrous, Lawrence K.   "Parody in Hawkes' The
           Lime Twig. " Critique (Atlanta) 15, no. 2 (1973):
           49-56.
           Explains how this work is a parody of both a
    thriller (or suspense story) and a mystery-detective

novel. Specifically, shows parody of the thriller's unified perspective and the usual "battle against inimical forces" and, following a description of the requisites of a mystery-detective novel, notes Hawkes's parody of these features by reversing them. Concludes by stating his perception of the novelist's reason for using parody in many of his works: "because it [parody] is the best vehicle with which to extend the form of the novel, creating at once an ambivalent world of destruction and hope."

529.   Edenbaum, Robert I. "John Hawkes: The Lime Twig and Other Tenuous Horrors." Massachusetts Review 7 (Summer 1966): 462-75.
        After noting some similarities among O'Connor, West, and Hawkes, states that both West and Hawkes insist "that the fantastic events of their novels have at their root sexual fantasy, both the 'worst dream and the best' of their characters." Briefly explains the use of fantasy in West's The Day of the Locust and then examines how human fantasy in The Lime Twig "accounts for his [man's] creativity as well as his destructiveness."
        Edenbaum next emphasizes the fantasies of Hencher and Banks and the part Larry plays in them, and he concludes with remarks upon the theme of violence and the vindication of humanity through childhood innocence in our present novel, the foundation of the book's violence on World War II visions, and the novel's redemptive finish.

530.   Fiedler, Leslie A. "A Lonely American Eccentric: The Pleasures of John Hawkes." New Leader, December 12, 1960, pp. 12-4; reprinted as "The Pleasures of John Hawkes." In The Cannibal, by John Hawkes, pp. vii-xiv. New York: New Directions, 1961; reprinted in his The Collected Essays of Leslie Fiedler, pp. 319-24. New York: Stein and Day, 1971; excerpted in Modern American Literature, pp. 50-1 (No. 587).
        "A lonely eccentric, a genuine unique ... John Hawkes ... is the least read novelist of substantial merit in the United States." This Gothic novelist carries us back to "the places in which we all live between sleeping and waking" and "makes terror rather than love the center of his work." In The Lime Twig he deals once again with "the immitigable mystery of

the world of common experience," where "love breed-
ing terror is itself the final terror." His poetic stylistic technique records our "untidy, half-focused, dis-
arrayed" consciousness but allows us some pleasure
through our knowledge of our irrational existence.

531.   Hassan, Ihab. "The Avant-Garde: Which Way Is For-
          ward?" Nation, November 18, 1961, pp. 396-9.
          [398-9]
          Expending but a few sentences on The Cannibal
and The Beetle Leg, Hassan offers a slightly longer
discussion of The Lime Twig. He designates the latter as "a story of love and evil," in which "the abom-
inations of desires come true and dreams become fact,"
and there is no sign of redemption.

531a.   _____. "The Character of Post-War Fiction in
          America." English Journal 51 (January 1962):
          1-8. [2, 6-7]
          Included in Hassan's list of contemporary Ameri-
can novels which manifest "that fusion of genres and
moods, that ambiguity of tone and attitude which is
characteristic of the age" are The Lime Twig and The
Cannibal. Added to these brief references are his
later comments on The Cannibal as "the most profound novel written about the last war" and on The
Lime Twig as a work whose unique style mitigates its
"nightmare world of evil."

531b.   Larsen, Erling. "The Shattering Controversial."
          Carleton Miscellany 3 (Winter 1962): 61-9. [64-
          6]
          Voices dislike for the movie, La Dolce Vita, and
also, apparently, for the book, The Lime Twig, a
novel "in the same tenor as that of the film," because
both supposedly are anti-realistic but offer pictures of
the horrendous realities of our world.

532.   Olderman, Raymond M. Beyond the Wasteland: A
          Study of the American Novel in the Nineteen-Six-
          ties. New Haven: Yale University Press, pp.
          150-75.
          Olderman analyzes this book as Hawkes's "explor-
ation of man's unconscious lust for death." He shows
how Hencher's memories and the desires of Michael
and Margaret, abetted by external random facts,
snare them into longing for death as a release

from the wasteland in which they exist, and points out
the importance of Larry, Sybelline, and Rock Castle
to this aspect of the story. He also delves into
Hawkes's use of suffering-child and bird images to
emphasize that the characters are "trapped and suffering victims"--symbols of man's helplessness in this
world. Finally, in remarking upon the novel's re-
demptive ending, Olderman appears to say that Hawkes,
like other black humor fabulists of the '60's, is anxious to affirm life no matter what the cost."

533.   Shepherd, Allen. "Illumination through (Anti)Climax:
        John Hawkes' The Lime Twig." Notes on Con-
        temporary Literature 2 (March 1972): 11-3.
        Discusses Hawkes's exploitation of the thriller
form to play upon "the reader's conventional expecta-
tion of literature and life" and thus often to mislead
the reader into expecting actions which never transpire.
But feels that the watchful reader is rewarded with an
expanded imagination and an appreciation of the irony
of the novel.

534.   Stubbs, John C. "John Hawkes and the Dream-World
        of The Lime Twig and Second Skin." Literature
        and Psychology 21 (1971): 149-60.
        By Hawkes's own admission his work attempts to
"force us ... to a recognition of the brutal longings
in the human psyche." Very powerful is this novelist's ability to mirror "man's psychic world," largely
through the use of "dream-distortion" in his scenes.
Indeed, The Lime Twig and Second Skin are best understood by looking at them as a series of anxiety
dreams. In the former, such a series primarily evidences struggles within the protagonists (Hencher,
Margaret, Michael) between the desire for power and
sensuous pleasure and a fear of these states, and,
secondarily, a "threatening of the individual sense of
security." In the latter, the threat to an individual's
--Skipper's--security is the primary theme. In both
books Hawkes uses images that link "physical power
with sexual potency."

535.   Warner, John M. "The 'Internalized Quest Romance'
        in Hawkes' The Lime Twig." Modern Fiction
        Studies 19 (Spring 1973): 89-95.
        Asserts that this novel is an exploration of the
possibilities and consequences of the artist's achieve-

ment of "imagination's freedom," the aim of the new
Romanticism. Details how the main emphasis of this
book is on the second of the two phases of the "internalized Romantic form of the archetypal quest," called
the phase of "the Real Man, the Imagination," in
which the prototypes of the artist-as-hero are found
in the characters Larry and Michael. Concludes that
the work is an "evolutionary document in the post-ro-
mantic effort to regenerate Blake's "Eternal Man."

SEE ALSO: Nos. 78, 83, 114, 554, 567, 570, 577-8, 581-
    4, 590-1, 593, 595, 597, 600, 602-3, 608-9, 611-
    3, 615, 617, 619.

Second Skin

536.   Galloway, David D. "Clown and Saint: the Hero in
            Current American Fiction." Critique (Atlanta) 7
            (Spring-Summer 1965): 46-65. [53-4]
        An unjustly overlooked writer of "great technical
virtuosity," Hawkes continues to display his talent for
"exposing the barrenness and brutality of the mass
mind as it slides ominously toward self-destruction or
gross inconsequence." His present novel gives us a
hero who survives despite being "the butt of everyone's worst sick joke," and whose second skin pos-
sesses a holiness suggestive of the more saintly
heroes of novels by Updike and Salinger.

537.   Graham, John, ed. The Merrill Studies in Second
            Skin. Columbus, Ohio: Charles E. Merrill,
            1971; paperback edition, Columbus, Ohio: Charles
            E. Merrill, 1971.
        A compendium of statements by Hawkes, reviews,
and critical pieces relating to this novel. Those items
previously published include reviews by Brooks (pp.
13-8; see No. 235), Kauffmann (pp. 5-8; see No. 256),
Ricks (pp. 9-12; see No. 269), Sontag (pp. 3-5; see
No. 275), and Wensberg (p. 2; see No. 282); Hawkes's
"Notes on The Wild Goose Chase," (pp. 20-3; see No.
58); "Story into Novel: [Introduction and] Commentary,"
and "The Nearest Cemetery" from Kuehl's book (pp.
35-8, 38-43; see Nos. 24, 61); excerpts from Enck's
and Graham's interviews with Hawkes (pp. 23-31, see
No. 78; pp. 31-3, see No. 83); and an essay by Over-
beck (pp. 45-52, see No. 606). Essays written ex-

pressly for this collection are:

a) Frost, Lucy, "Awakening Paradise," pp. 52-
63, which discusses the coherence of this novel,
brought about by recurring images and action;

b) Robinson, William, "John Hawkes' Artificial
Inseminator," pp. 63-9, which notes Hawkes's deliberate display of his "self-conscious literariness,"
dependent upon many literary correlates, in this book;

c) Nichols, Stephen G., "Vision and Tradition in
Second Skin," pp. 69-82, which speaks of Hawkes's
imaginative vision and how it appears in Second Skin
through an interaction between his private vision and
the "whole cultural tradition of Western literature";

d) Santore, Anthony C, "Narrative Unreliability
and the Structure of Second Skin," pp. 83-93, which
suggests that an understanding of Hawkes's use of the
unreliable narrator, a literary device that reaches as
far back as Irving, Melville, and Hawthorne in the
American tradition, allows the reader to appreciate
the comedy and suggestion of hope found in the book;
and

e) Guerard, Albert J., "Second Skin: the Light
and the Dark Affirmation," pp. 93-102, which finds
this work to be a "serene Tempest," having as its
theme the conquest of private catastrophe, discusses
the imagery and symbolism (especially the recurring
voyeuristic patterns), and compares Hawkes with Nabokov and Bellow.

538.   Greiner, Donald J.   "The Thematic Use of Color in
        John Hawkes' Second Skin." Contemporary Lit-
        erature 11 (Summer 1970): 389-400.
        Explaining that structure "based on cross-refer-
ences, parallels, and contrasts" is often the key to
Hawkes's works, Greiner finds the structure of this
novel to be dependent on color imagery, used "themat-
ically to provide a frame of reference for fragmentary, often motiveless action and for the violent time
shifts." He says that the most prominent variations
are on the colors green, yellow, black, and white,
and interprets what each color means with respect to
Skipper's locale. For, the symbolism generally
changes, in Greiner's opinion, with certain changes in
locale, with the exception of the final chapter, in
which many of the motifs are drawn together "to cele-
brate Skipper's victory over pain, horror, and death."

539.   Guerard, Albert J.   "The Illuminating Distortion. "
            Novel 5 (Winter 1972):   101-21.   [115]
            Maintains that Hawkes's treatment of man's "for-
        bidden wishes and games, " depending on his fresh and
        powerful language, achieves peculiar comic, often
        parodic, effects and intense, terrifying scenes.   Men-
        tions briefly in this regard the homosexual allusions
        in both Second Skin and The Blood Oranges and the
        father-daughter incest undertone of the former work
        and the mate-swapping of the latter.

540.   Imhoff, Ron.   "On Second Skin. "   Mosaic 8 (Fall
            1974):   51-63.
            By applying Mukarovsky's theory of literary struc-
        ture to the structure of Second Skin Imhoff locates
        "foregrounding, " or the distortion of the traditional
        fictional devices of plot, character, setting, and theme
        in the chapter, "The Brutal Act, " and designates the
        highly marked murder scene within this chapter as
        the dominant scene of the book.   He explains that
        with this chapter Hawkes emphasizes his "rejection of
        conventional fiction, " but that the recurrences of the
        three parts of the chapter "constitute the 'coherence'
        of Hawkes' imaginative fiction. "   He states, in addi-
        tion, that the unconventional structure is also moti-
        vated by Skipper's refusal to recall the murder scene
        and his wish to accentuate his "blameless impotence."
            Hawkes's two-page response to Imhoff, attached
        to this article, concerns his intention to make Skipper
        a culpable narrator, his definition of innocence, and
        his denial of either his or Skipper's "concerned de-
        tachment. "   His concluding words divulge Skipper's
        humanity and his new novel's (Death, Sleep & the
        Traveler) "insistence on the necessity to accept noth-
        ingness. "

541.   Lavers, Norman.   "The Structure of Second Skin. "
            Novel 5 (Spring 1972):   208-14.
            Poses the idea that in this book Hawkes is paro-
        dying The Great American Novel.   Demonstrates what
        characteristics of the American novel as theorized by
        Richard Chase (The American Novel and Its Tradi-
        tions) and Leslie Fiedler (Love and Death in the
        American Novel) this work has and, in line with
        Chase's belief that the American novel contains a
        strong element of romance, interprets this novel as
        a romance in the tradition of Daphnis and Chloe and

The Golden Ass. Dwells especially on the romantic
"alternation between 'melodramatic action' and 'pastoral idyl'." Also indicates Skipper's position as a
symbolic Christ figure--a necessary element in American fiction.

542.   LeClair, Thomas (Edmund). "John Hawkes's 'Death
        of an Airman' and Second Skin." Notes on Con-
        temporary Literature 4 (January 1974): 2-3.
        Holds that the symbolic act of Skipper's lying in
a hearse in Second Skin is based on a similar scene
in Hawkes's earlier story, "Death of an Airman," and
that both works share a common theme--the relationship of death and innocence. Considers, further, that
this act indicates the falsity of Skipper's innocence
and the destruction of really innocent people through
this false innocence.

543.   _____. "The Unreliability of Innocence: John
        Hawkes' Second Skin." Journal of Narrative
        Technique 3 (January 1973): 32-9.
        Finding the theme of death and innocence to exist
in all of Hawkes's novels, LeClair speaks specifically
of the novelist's pursuit of this theme in Second Skin
through skilful use of the unreliable narrator, Skipper.
He feels that Skipper's "ironic self-revelation" ex-
poses mankind's weakness of "disability, inadequacy
[and] hypocrisy, all covered with a veneer of ingenu-
ous innocence" and, by maintaining a tension between
the reader's scorn and sympathy for the revealer, allows the meaning of innocence to be continually ex-
amined in the novel. Exploring Skipper's relationship
with his mother, wife, and daughter, he shows how
Skipper clutches a "perverse self-willed innocence"
and represses the reality of death. Finally, he sees
a similarity between this novel's treatment of innocence and that of the traditional 19th-century American novel and wonders, too, if Skipper's survival is
ironic or affirmative.

544.   Lucie-Smith, Edward. "American Needs." Sunday
        Times (London), November 7, 1965, p. 51.
        States in a handful of sentences that like Bellow's
Herzog this work portrays a "middle-aged man in
search of himself" and concerns itself with "the sub-
jective experience of the individual." Comments that
the latter concern discontents many readers because

of the avoidance of issues covered by the new satirists.

545. Pearce, Richard. Stages of the Clown; Perspectives on Modern Fiction from Dostoyevsky to Beckett. Carbondale: Southern Illinois University Press, 1970, pp. 102-16.
      Interprets Bellow's narrator in Henderson the Rain King and Skipper in Hawkes's present work as clowns in the tradition of Harlequin, one of four archetypal clown figures described by Pearce in this volume. Explains that both novels hold death at their centers and that, like Harlequin, both hero/narrators realize that "war is the condition of life" and accept their role as clown. With respect to Hawkes's work, discloses further that Skipper reveals the "contradiction of modern man's psychological reality" through the novel's style and a "kaleidoscopic structure," which interlaces three major patterns.

546. Yarborough, Richard. "Hawkes' Second Skin." Mosaic 8 (Fall 1974): 65-75.
      In making analogies between this work and the literary forms of poetry and drama first points out the novel's similarities to Berryman's The Dream Songs concerning the "overwhelming influence of the paternal suicide" and the lyrical visions and immaturity of the narrators. Next, provides interpretations of Second Skin's major images--male, female, and island--continuing on to find in the novel's inclusion of fate and portrayal of Skipper as a tragic hero a likeness to classical tragedy. Proclaims, in conclusion, that Skipper survives through his artful rendering of his life's story, just as Berryman advocated in his poetry.
      Hawkes's two-page response to Yarborough's article on pages 63-5 concerns mythologizing death in and the religiousness of his fiction and his understanding of detachment.

SEE ALSO: Nos. 63, 66, 70, 83, 114, 534, 567, 570, 577-8, 583, 590-1, 593, 595-6, 600, 613, 615, 617.

The Blood Oranges

547. Cuddy, Lois A. "Functional Pastoralism in The Blood Oranges." Studies in American Fiction 3 (Spring 1975): 15-25.

Greater appreciation for this novel is gained by
analysis of Hawkes's use of pastoralism, and especially his adaptation of pastoral conventions, in consider-
ing the structural and conceptual essence of the book.
We find that the feature of "pastoral opposition" is
presented through the various characters and images,
epitomized in the "polarities of life styles, modes of
thought, and perception" of Hugh and Cyril. Moreover, pathos and pastoral conflict appear to arise
from integrating the two pastoral ideals known as the
"pastoral of innocence" and the "pastoral of happiness."
        This novel, a "unique pastoral elegy" based on the
concepts of fidelity and friendship, can even be seen
as a variation of the funeral elegy. However, it
shows itself, ultimately, to be a "pastoral of the self."
        Cyril, Hugh, and Fiona can all be viewed, finally,
as important pastoral figures, if not "different ver-
sions of pastoral man." The implication is that we
too, might all be potentially pastoral men; for Hawkes
does seem to challenge us to reassess our conventional values and approaches to life.

548.   Knapp, John V. "Hawkes' The Blood Oranges: a
        Sensual New Jerusalem." Critique (Atlanta) 17,
        no. 3 (1976): 5-25.
        With the firm belief that this is "an intensely mor-
al and beautifully lyrical novel" which owes much to
Plato's Symposium and Phaedrus, Milton's Lycidas,
the Bible, Twelfth Night, the works of a few other authors, and flower symbology, and that Hawkes is attempting "to create a 'new' morality to supplant the
outworn asexuality of a moribund Christianity," Knapp
studies the imagery, tone, and meaning of several important scenes to prove these theses.

SEE ALSO: Nos. 70, 74, 81, 92, 114, 539, 567, 570, 578,
        583, 590, 593, 596.

Death, Sleep & the Traveler

549.   Greiner, Donald J. "Death, Sleep & the Traveler:
        John Hawkes' Return to Terror." Critique (At-
        lanta) 17, no. 3 (1976): 26-38.
        Viewing this work as a return to pure terror,
tempered in no way by comedy, Greiner suggests that

Allert, a possible schizophrenic or insane murderer,
dreams the entire novel and in this dream attempts
to prove the validity of the statement that a man
loses his virginity only when he has murdered some-
one.   He briefly explores the symbols of the sea and
ocean liner to show their reference to Allert's
dreamworld and psyche and argues through several il-
lustrations that the other characters of the novel are
merely projections of Allert's mind.   Greiner calcu-
lates that in its evocation of sexuality this is Hawkes's
most erotic novel but also that it presents nearly de-
ranged sexual fantasies, including the equation of
sterility and sex and sex and death.

·550.   Kraus, Elisabeth.   "Psychic Sores in Search of Compassion: Hawkes' Death, Sleep & the Traveler."
Critique (Atlanta) 17, no. 3 (1976): 39-52.
Builds an argument that, as in previous novels,
Hawkes here dramatizes the "conflict between man's
instinctual needs and the repressive customs and conventions of our civilization."   Pictures Allert as a
homosexual whose wish to become an "artist" through
sexual activity has to be repressed and vented only in
imagination and in retreat to a dream world.   Shows
this repression to be the cause of Allert's violent dis-
posal of Ariane, at the very least.   In the final paragraph defends the novel against some critical reviews
and lauds Hawkes's "stylistic power."

SEE ALSO: Nos. 70, 81, 84, 540, 561, 590, 596.

Travesty

See No. 89.

B.   SHORT FICTION (excluding the novellas) see no. 542,
567-8, 582-3.

C.   PLAYS

551.   Blau, Herbert.   Preface to The Innocent Party, by
John Hawkes.   New York: New Directions,
[1967] c1966, pp. 9-12.
Impressed with Hawkes's observation of and par-

ticipation in the work of his Actor's Workshop in San
Francisco, Blau voices his admiration of the novelist
and praises his exuberant treatment of "dead passions"
in all of his works.   With respect to the plays he
comments on their inclusion of "an inscape of wonder
in a landscape of mutilations" and their positioning of
innocence "on the limb, ripe for perversion." He
feels strongly that the plays "sing" and are "worth
imagining in the theater."

552.   Cohn, Ruby. Dialogue in American Drama. Bloom-
            ington: Indiana University Press, 1971, pp. 198-
            201; excerpted in Contemporary Literary Criticism,
            p. 215 (No. 586).
        All of Hawkes's plays share the same theme--the
lustful and violent "decline of white Protestant America"--a like implication "that reality consists of improvised motives accumulating into a role," and a
similar construction, in which "a shocking confronta-
tion mounts in intensity to an ambiguous finale."
The Innocent Party and The Wax Museum both dramatize "a development from solitude to togetherness."
The Undertaker, designated a "farcical melodrama" by
Hawkes, loses some fictional intensity and mystery because of its farcical effects.   The Questions arrives
at theatrical urgency through constant suggestive questioning.

553.   Weales, Gerald. The Jumping-Off Place: American
            Drama in the 1960's. New York: Macmillan,
            1969, pp. 208-11; excerpted in Contemporary Lit-
            erary Criticism, p. 213 (No. 586).
        Hawkes's plays suggest more than they define and
depict a world of "matter-of-fact grotesqueness, in which
blood and lust are staples ... and innocence is for-
ever menaced." The best of these largely verbal
plays is The Questions, whose effectiveness, as with
Pinter's The Homecoming, depends upon "an obvious
struggle" and whose language is fascinating.   The other
plays lack dramatic substance, and more specifically,
The Undertaker and The Wax Museum are just "clever
pieces."

SEE ALSO: Nos. 95, 570.

D.   LECTURES/READINGS

554.   Beck, Ellen.   "Hawkes: Fiction."   McGill Daily
        (Montreal), October 23, 1970, p. 1.
            Utilizing several quotations from Hawkes, pro-
        vides a short description of a lecture given by the
        novelist at McGill on October 22, 1970.   The topics
        included are Hawkes's theory of fiction, use of land-
        scape and comedy, and the origin of the title of The
        Lime Twig.

555.   Brill, Maggie.   "Hawkes Sees Moral Issue as Vital
        to New Writers."   Justice (Waltham, Mass.),
        October 20, 1959, p. 2.
            Hawkes's lecture on "The New Novelists in Amer-
        ica," delivered at Brandeis University on October 14,
        1959, is described.   Quoted are Hawkes's comments
        on the novelists' necessary treatment of the question
        of evil, his exclusion of the Beat Generation from the
        definition of novelist, and the definition and purpose
        of the anti-realist.

556.   Jacobs, Joanne.   "Imagination, Sexuality: Hawkes
        Emphasizes Vision."   Stanford Daily, November
        16, 1973, p. 8.
            An article comprised mainly of statements select-
        ed from those made by Hawkes during the Modern
        Thought and Literature Conference at Stanford Univer-
        sity.   The paraphrases and quotations concern such
        topics as the relationship between imagination and sex-
        ual life, pornography as "the ordinary man's art,"
        Hawkes's attempt to "further the form of literature"
        in which he is writing, what students and others need
        and expect from fiction, and how fiction differs from
        non-fiction.

557.   Knopp, Peter.   "Hawkes Analyzes Anti-realism in His
        Own Novel, Beetle Egg [sic]."   Brown Daily Her-
        ald, January 13, 1960, p. 1.
            Concerns Hawkes's remarks as a guest lecturer
        in an English class at Brown on the characteristics of
        the anti-realistic novel and on the " 'anti-realism' of
        novels of the past twenty years."   Provides brief quo-
        tations from Hawkes on The Beetle Leg, The Day of
        the Locust, and The Velvet Horn.

558.   McGarry, Jean.   "John Hawkes: Exposing Life As a

Comic." <u>Pawtucket Times</u>, May 17, 1974, p. 22.
Accompanied by a short excerpt from <u>Second Skin</u>,
describes a reading given by Hawkes at Brown.   Beginning with a discussion of Hawkes's unique brand of
comedy, follows, thereafter, with some details on the
novelist's career and writings and several quotations
from the reading, including the novelist's acknowledg-
ment that "he has been writing variations on a single
character in all his work."

559.   Menn, Thorpe.   "Literature Seen As Test for Evoking
          Compassion."   <u>Kansas City Times</u>, January 19,
          1966, p. 7.
          Menn summarizes comments made by Hawkes
while speaking before a small but enthusiastic group
at the local Jewish Community Center.   He notes
Hawkes's insistence that "everyone lives in a nightmare" and that literature has as one of its purposes
the testing of our capacity for compassion.

560.   Simon, Jeff.   "John Hawkes Reads Imaginative Works
          for Audience at UB."   <u>Buffalo Evening News</u>,
          April 21, 1972, p. 18.
          Naming Hawkes "one of the most gifted and ac-
complished writers of prose fiction in America," Simon writes about Hawkes's reading and discussion of
his works at the State University at Buffalo.   He
stresses the importance of the imagination in the novelist's fiction and quotes some of Hawkes's remarks on
his novels and how they have been interpreted and received by others.

*561.   Willis, Judith.   "John Hawkes: Terror and Joy."
          <u>Woodwind</u> 4 (January 30, 1973).
          Contributes comments on the essence and some of
the highlights of Hawkes's presentation at one of the
Folger Poetry Readings, in which the novelist devoted
most of his time to "pursuing an image" through three
of his novels and, in doing so, pointed up his "comic
vision" and disclosed some of the inspirations for
<u>Death, Sleep & the Traveler</u>.

562.   Young, Barbara.   "John Hawkes and the 'Cut of the
          Absurd'."   <u>Justice</u> (Waltham, Mass.), February
          22, 1955, p. 4.
          Ms. Young talks about a lecture given by Hawkes
at Brandeis on the "aesthetics and aims" of his form

of fiction writing, beginning with a few sentences noting
the novelist's defense of his art. Then, however, after a lengthy explanation of the meaning of "the Absurd" over the years, she calls Hawkes, a member
of the New Avant Garde, a practitioner of the art of
the Lesser Absurdist movements of the past--"an art
of pure technical virtuosity and personal uncommit-
ment." Her closing remarks, including quotations
from Davis (see No. 131) on The Cannibal, all concern the meaninglessness and incomprehensibility of
such works as Hawkes writes.

E. GENERAL CRITICISM

563.   Barth, John. "A Tribute to John Hawkes." Harvard
         Advocate 104 (October 1970): 11.
         "In the landscape of our fiction he [Hawkes] stands
improbably as Gibraltar: unaccountable, astonishing,
formidable, sui generis, and self-sufficient, at once
familiar and exotic...." Creator of difficult but beautiful works, Hawkes displays his "singularity and chief
richness" in his "telling voice." "There is not one
[contemporary American writer] I more admire."

564.   Baumbach, Jonathan. The Landscape of Nightmare:
         Studies in the Contemporary American Novel.
         New York: New York University Press, 1965, p.
         5; excerpted in Contemporary Literary Criticism,
         p. 212 (No. 586).
         In a lengthy footnote to his text Baumbach refers
to Hawkes's out-of-focus landscapes that confront and
envelop us like nightmares or "workaday evil
dream[s]." He views Hawkes's novels as "so many
eccentric exercises."

565.   Blaise, Clark. "Notes: On Hawkes." McGill Daily
         (Montreal), October 16, 1970, The Supplement
         section, p. 5.
         Readily admits Hawkes's continual obscurity and
difficulty of his works. Explains the primacy of
place in the novelist's fictions--"a place that engulfs
the action and perception of the characters"--and notes,
as well, the unconventional nature of his characters.
Perceiving Hawkes's concentration on structure, feels
that, like the creations of Borges, Beckett and Berg-

man, Hawkes's are examples of "sophisticated art,"
so perfect as not to require meaning.

566.   Brimble, Phillip S. "Writer Uses Bizarre to Clari-
            fy." Kansas City Times, January 15, 1966, p.
            28.
        Written just prior to Hawkes's appearance before
a local community group, this brief article basically
provides a few biographical facts about the novelist,
quotes Hawkes on his fictive concerns and treatment
of violence, and presents short quotes by Flannery
O'Connor and Webster Schott on Hawkes's work.

567.   Brodin, Pierre. "John Hawkes." Informations &
            Documents, No. 317 (April 1972), pp. 24-7; re-
            printed in his Continuateurs et novateurs; Ecrivains
            américains d'aujourdhui, pp. 149-56.   Présences
            contemporaines.   Paris: Nouvelles Editions De-
            bresse, 1973.
        Outlines Hawkes's novels through 1971 but spends
more time on The Cannibal and on The Lime Twig.
Considers Spitzen-on-the-Dein of the former to be a
microcosm of our perenially violent world, and the
characters of the latter, a surrealistic gothic novel,
to be quite lifelike in their torment and suffering.
Finds Second Skin to portray a man's victory over des-
tiny and death, Lunar Landscapes to be filled with
symbolic obsessions and nightmarish allegories, and
The Blood Oranges to be more than the romantic dream
of a narcissistic narrator.   Finally, praises Hawkes
as a great artist and as "un grand musicien du Verbe"
(a great musician with speech).

568.   _____. "Roman laboratoire: la Littérature expéri-
            mentale." Informations & Documents, No. 291
            (March 1-15 1970), pp. 38-43. [39, 41]
        Several lengthy sentences are devoted to Hawkes
in this article on a dozen or so American experimental novelists.   Alluded to as uniquely his are his trans-
formations of ordinary happenings into those of terror,
although his cruel lucidity ("une lucidité cruelle") is
thought to be not unlike that of Burroughs.   On the other hand, his violence is considered to be more restrained and his nightmares more subtle than these
same features in Burroughs' works.   The surrealistic
attributes of both The Cannibal and Lunar Landscapes
are briefly touched upon, also.

569.   Burgess, Anthony. "On Lengthy Matters." New
           York Times Book Review, December 14, 1975,
           p. 39.
           In criticizing the excessive length of most con-
        temporary American novels Burgess specifically hails
        "all the works of John Hawkes," among the novels of
        a few other authors, as examples of the "really great
        American novels" that have all been rather short.

570.   Busch, Frederick. Hawkes: A Guide to His Fictions.
           Syracuse: Syracuse University Press, 1973.
           The first full-length study of Hawkes's major
        works to have been published and still the only one to
        present a chronological work-by-work, close exposi-
        tion, stressing "lyrical and baroque language." Point-
        ed out first are Charivari's parody and animal images
        --key features of all the works. Next, The Cannibal
        is described as "a Jacobean triumph," merging "bril-
        liant stylistics and social concern." Dense animal
        imagery, "adorning the theme of sterility and hopeless-
        ness," and mythic elements are found in The Beetle
        Leg, while The Owl is held to have an "overriding
        sense of death and futility" and The Goose on the
        Grave, that of "disaster and victimization."
           Hawkes's attainment to first-rank status among
        modern novelists is proclaimed as The Lime Twig's
        carefully-constructed images, compelling characters,
        and "masterful use of first-person narrator" are dis-
        cussed. Further, Second Skin is unveiled as a "tri-
        umph of structure and language" with its "contrapunt-
        ally-structured narrative"; The Innocent Party, as show-
        ing a concern for "basic American social and histori-
        cal material"; and The Blood Oranges, as unrolling a
        "dialectic between time and timelessness."

571.   Davis, Douglas M. "The New Mood: An Obsession
           with the Absurd." National Observer, February
           15, 1965, p. 22.
           Concerns several contemporary American writers,
        including Hawkes, all of whom are said to be "ob-
        sessed with the absurd side of American life" and to
        be exhibiting profound nihilism in their work. Names
        Hawkes as the earliest practitioner of this "new
        mood," although mentioning his anonymity, resulting
        from his difficult, but challenging, prose and almost
        surrealistic landscapes. Adds that Hawkes intends to
        continue writing in his unique manner and thus to con-

tinue his reflection of the nightmarish world in which
we live.

572.   "Desiat' populiarnykh v knigoizdatel'skom mire pista-
        lei" [Ten Popular Writers in the Publishing
        World]. Amerika, No. 127 (May 1967), pp. 4-5. [5]
        Among the ten writers who are treated individual-
ly in short paragraphs Hawkes is cited as having become known as the contemporary Edgar Allan Poe.
His surrealistic form, gothic nightmarishness, and ex-
istentialistic hope are noted, and his aim in showing
and attacking the evil in man is quoted.

573.   Ekner, Reidar. "Den säregne Hawkes" [Hawkes the
        Strange]. Dagens Nyheter (Stockholm), July 11,
        1955, p. 3.
        Ekner concerns himself with Hawkes's work in
general and provides expanded comments on four novels in particular. Calling Charivari an uninteresting
surrealistic nightmare, he nonetheless praises The
Cannibal for its outstanding dramatic power and scenic
observations and follows this with applause for The
Beetle Leg as a virtuoso study in psychological or
physiological stagnation and The Owl as a novella of
archaic, forceful language. He observes that Hawkes's
peculiar treatment of time is consonant with the novelist's style of writing and that the macabre elements
are made more palatable by being expressed in the
language of a literary craftsman. Also briefly treating Hawkes's development of mystical heroes and aim
of depicting man's struggle against the evil, fear, and
loneliness of the past, he concludes by affirming
Hawkes's position as the most original and most sure
of young American authors.

574.   "Fiction's Cutting Edge." Catalyst (Colorado Springs),
        May 3, 1974, p. 6.
        Announcing the advent of a writer's conference at
Colorado College on recent American fiction, notes
Hawkes's participation in the festival and, in a few
sentences, characterizes Hawkes's work as "poetic,
beautiful and terrifying," as well as comic.

575.   Foster, Geraldine S. "The Philosophy of John Hawkes."
        Rhode Island Herald (Pawtucket), February 11, 1966,
        pp. 18-9.
        Ms. Foster offers thoughts taken from her under-

graduate paper on Hawkes. She covers the typical
qualities of a Hawkes novel, including the grotesque
characters, the barren landscapes, the lack of conventional reality, and a "precise, taut language that
captivates and dazzles," and holds, as several others
do, that one participates in a Hawkes novel rather
than reads it. However, she disagrees emphatically
with what she considers is the novelist's view of life:
existence in a "godless universe at whose core one
discovers only terror, darkness, and a tremendous
reservoir of violence."

576.   Friedman, Melvin J. "John Hawkes and Flannery O'-
        Connor: the French Background." Boston Uni-
        versity Journal 21 (Fall 1973): 34-44.
        Hawkes's experimentalism, "infatuation with
words," and reliance on first-person narrative are
initially contrasted with O'Connor's comparatively conventional style and constant use of the third person.
Yet after Hawkes's similarity to French writer-critics
like Robbe-Grillet is established and his "Notes on
The Wild Goose Chase" is briefly discussed, similarities between the work of both authors are touched upon: their modification of the picaresque, use of
"landscapes of violence," repetitions, and lifeless spa-
tial images, a fascination with physical objects, and
an enjoyment of "playing with such opposites as innocence and perversion, the sacred and the sexual."
A final tribute to both authors for undertaking to
change the shape of the novel is also made.

576a.   Frohock, W. M. "The Dilemmas of Criticism."
        Southwest Review 46 (Summer 1961): 205-14.
        [211]
        As an example of the "divorce between critical
and 'creative' functioning" among contemporary American writers, Frohock cites the instance of the total
lack of comment (up to that time) by John Hawkes and
Edwin Honig, longtime friends and colleagues, on
each other's work.

577.   _____. "John Hawkes's Vision of Violence."
        Southwest Review 50 (Winter 1965): 69-79.
        Following a demonstration of the kinds of plots
used in Hawkes's novels, in which The Cannibal, The
Lime Twig, and Second Skin are used as examples,
Frohock talks extensively about the novelist's tech-

nique of secretiveness--i. e. , his suppression of information normally given to the reader--in the realm of
motive and especially of perspective. He also considers Hawkes's unique "vision of violence," which is
really a "vision of life's not always lovely potentiali-
ties." Frohock believes that Hawkes has succeeded
in doing something new with the novel form by allowing his readers to follow "a hypersensitive imagination as it faces the fact of existence."

577a.   Greengrass, E. E. "Studying Hawkes." Open Letter,
         ser. 3, No. 2 (Fall 1975), pp. 112-4.   +
         This is a critique of Greiner's book (see No. 578)
which disagrees with Greiner's designation of Hawkes
as a Black Humorist, laments his repetitious introduction, odd sentence structure, and contradictory remarks concerning Hawkes as a moralist, and most
importantly, believes that he has not justly treated
Hawkes's language or accurately assessed Hawkes's
novels as poetic works. Greengrass not only views
Hawkes as a "determined and genuine experimenter"
but also as a writer who "shares a lot with contemporary avant-garde poetry." He even notes similarities
between Hawkes's statements about his writing and
those voiced by Pound, William Carlos Williams, and
Yeats.

578.   Greiner, Donald J. Comic Terror: the Novels of
        John Hawkes. Memphis: Memphis State Univer-
        sity Press, 1973.
        This latest monographic treatment of Hawkes's
works aims primarily at clarifying Hawkes's technique
and use of comedy and at placing Hawkes's humor into perspective. The introductory chapter discusses
the similarity of Hawkes's aim to that of other black
humorists, notes, in general terms, the novelist's
avoidance of conventional devices of realism in preference of poetic techniques and his concern for structural coherence, and finally, delineates Hawkes's un-
traditional brand of comedy. (Greiner first presented
the last argument in an article which appears in this
bibliography as No. 579.)
        In the chapters which follow, Greiner analyzes
each of Hawkes's fictional works through The Blood
Oranges with respect to intent, technique, and comedy
and attempts to interpret some of the more difficult
parts of these works. The concluding chapter once

again emphasizes the novelist's break with realism and the use of comedy but argues as well that Hawkes has gradually moved towards realism and offers in his later works a "more accessible reading experience and a more recognizable humor."

579.   . "Strange Laughter: the Comedy of John Hawkes." Southwest Review 56 (Autumn 1971): 318-28; excerpted in Contemporary Literary Criticism, p. 214 (No. 586).
After presenting some well-known theories of comedy, demonstrates how and why Hawkes's brand of comedy does not adhere to any of them. Indicates Hawkes's repudiation of traditional comedy's acceptance of a social standard implying stability and uniformity of behavior, contrasts the novelist's interpretation of the "humanely malign comic spirit" with that of Meredith, and states his violation of Bergson's long-accepted separation of comedy and emotion. Discusses Hawkes's novels as "comedies of the inappropriate response," as well as "comedies of nightmare." Concludes with reflections upon the reader's difficulties with Hawkes's, and modern comedy's, humor--difficulties arising from the use of terrifying events which nonetheless produce laughter, the demand for recognition of "the terrifying gulfs within man, and between men," and the suggestion of hope despite the violence.

580. Guerard, Albert J. "Introduction to the Cambridge Anti-Realists." Audience 7 (Spring 1960): 57-9.
Numbers Hawkes among the Cambridge Anti-Realists, a group of writers who especially find "positive pleasure and value in frank grotesque distortion, in black humour and fantasy, [and] in a personal recreation of the visible and the inner world" and who reflect somewhat man's modern drive towards annihilation. Feels that Hawkes, though more conscious and controlled than in earlier days, still evokes "another world behind the world we think we see."

581.   . "The Prose Style of John Hawkes." Critique (Atlanta) 6 (Fall 1963): 19-29.
Guerard analyzes a few aspects of the development of Hawkes's style ("one of the most personal of contemporary prose styles"), along with some continuing characteristics of that style. He discusses the

writer's gradual adoption of a less exuberantly inventive style and a diminishing of his early penchant for "literary" display and reflects upon the growth of a "terrifying" kind of irony and control in Hawkes's works.   In speaking of voice he notes the difference between Hawkes's narrators, concentrating largely on the modulations of tone in The Lime Twig.   His concluding statement highlights Hawkes's powerful renditions of "uncensored revelry," "violent fantasy," and "pullulant underground life," with great stylistic control.

582.   Hassan, Ihab. "American Literature." In World
         Literature Since 1945; Critical Surveys of the
         Contemporary Literature of Europe and the Amer-
         icas, p. 15.   Edited by Ivar Ivask and Gero von
         Wilpert. New York: F. Ungar, 1973.
         Basically, a shortened version of the following
       item (No. 583).

583.   _____. Contemporary American Literature, 1945-
         1972; an Introduction.   New York: F. Ungar,
         1973, pp. 52-4.
         Finds in Hawkes's work a dominant gothic strain,
       a satirical impulse, and a precise surrealism which
       clarify the inner life of man.   Provides a few ex-
       amples of the novelist's "angle of vision," focusing
       as it does on grisly, insidious happenings, and ex-
       plains that Hawkes's innate weakness--overly retro-
       gressive and discrete language--was overcome in Sec-
       ond Skin.   However, considers Hawkes's art and ex-
       ploration of man's emotions to be too narrow and the
       subtleties of The Blood Oranges "merely aspects of
       poetic virtuosity."

584.   _____. "The Dial and Recent American Fiction."
         CEA Critic 29 (October 1966): 1, 3.
         In a few phrases describes Hawkes's works (spe-
       cifically, The Cannibal and The Lime Twig) as gothic
       novels which "depict the mournful frolics of terror and
       nightmare" and push "negative transcendence" (the act
       by which intelligence tries to subvert itself) towards
       the goal of hell.   Also maintains that Hawkes is con-
       cerned with the violence of apocalypse.

585.   "Hawkes, John." In Encyclopedia of World Literature
         in the 20th Century, v. 2, p. 95.   General editor:

Wolfgang Bernard Fleischmann. New York: Ungar, 1967.
A short paragraph on the characteristics of Hawkes's works, including the novelist's utilization of "sadistic-masochistic rhythms of the unconscious as a structural and thematic principle." Lists some of Hawkes's writings and three bibliographical references.

586. "Hawkes, John, 1925- ." In Contemporary Literary Criticism; Excerpts from the Criticism of Works of Today's Novelists, Poets, Playwrights, and Other Creative Writers, v. 4, pp. 212-9. Edited by Carolyn Riley. Detroit: Gale Research Co., 1975.
Twenty-one excerpts from books, articles, and reviews concerned with Hawkes's work. Most are quite lengthy and are important, recent (1969-74) items. In this bibliography each of these excerpts is noted along with the original piece when the original is cited.

587. "Hawkes, John (1925-)." In Modern American Literature, v. 2, pp. 49-54. A Library of Literary Criticism. Compiled and edited by Dorothy Nyren Curley, Maurice Kramer, and Elaine Fialka. 4th enlarged edition. New York: Ungar, 1969.
Excerpts from thirteen early major reviews and critical articles on Hawkes's work. In this bibliography each excerpt is noted along with the original piece when the original is cited.

588. Horovitz, Israel. "Les Inconnus, les espoirs." Le Magazine littéraire, No. 66 (July-August 1972), p. 65. (Translated by Jean-Paul Delamotte.)
Reflects upon the fact that Hawkes is still considered a "young writer," despite his lengthy, enviable writing career, because he is largely unread. Fears that Hawkes's work may never become more popular since solid barriers to that popularity have been erected by the novelist's concentration on style.

589. "James Laughlin." Informations & Documents, No. 187 (September 15-October 1, 1963), pp. 34-5.
In talking about several of the writers he has published Laughlin voices his regard for Hawkes by calling him a replacement for Faulkner. Proclaiming Hawkes a genius, he declares the novelist's works to

have great significance and psychological implications.

590.   Klein, Marcus. "Hawkes in Love." Annals de la
       Faculté des Lettres et Sciences humaines de Tou-
       louse: Caliban 12, n. s. 11 (1975): 65-79.
           "The most unremittingly artistic novelist in Amer-
       ica," Hawkes, though insisting on the detachment of
       his created work from any outside, actual event, does
       draw upon "outward event and historical circumstance"
       and really contradicts his aim of detachment by advo-
       cating, in addition, the satiric function of novel-writ-
       ing. Moreover, the materials of Hawkes's novels re-
       fuse to be contained within their form and therefore,
       give the reader difficulty. Yet Hawkes produces suc-
       cessful visions by aptly combining devices of stasis
       with those of disruption (the latter called "vital ma-
       rauders"). Second Skin, The Blood Oranges, and
       Death, Sleep & the Traveler, Hawkes's love novels,
       provide especially good examples of this artistic tech-
       nique.

591.   _____. "John Hawkes' Experimental Compositions."
       In Surfiction; Fiction Now ··· and Tomorrow, pp.
       203-14. Edited by Raymond Federman. Chicago:
       Swallow Press, 1975.
           An earlier version of the previous article (No.
       590), which makes no mention of The Blood Oranges
       or Death, Sleep & the Traveler. Thus, it ends with
       an extended look at Second Skin, showing how it ap-
       pears to be written from a "perspective of mellowed
       comic wisdom" but actually contains the same horrors
       as any other Hawkesian novel and a conclusion that
       results from the typical Hawkesian vision of death.

592.   Klinkowitz, Jerome and Somer, John, eds. Innovative
       Fiction: Stories for the Seventies. New York:
       Dell, 1972, pp. xxiv-xxv.
           The "Introduction" fleetingly talks of Hawkes's
       stylistic techniques of casting aside plot and develop-
       ing works which give insight into "the psychic nature
       of the experience," as well as the novelist's purpose
       in undertaking "the Voice Project."

593.   Kuehl, John. John Hawkes and the Craft of Conflict.
       New Brunswick, N. J.: Rutgers University Press,
       1975.
           In this recent study of Hawkes's work Kuehl dem-

onstrates the evolution and relationship of the novelist's central theme--the tension between Eros and
Thanatos--and style by focusing on the formal patterns
of "landscape and settings, myths and rituals, structure, characterization, and narrative focus." While
speaking of Hawkes's warscapes, lovescapes, etc., he
especially emphasizes the identification of external nature, which is noxious and uncontrollable, with human
nature. He covers Hawkes's parody and use of myth
and offers comments also on the negative treatment of
religious rituals, a pre-1960 "mythopoetic vision of
reality," and a post-1960 move towards conventional
structure, resulting from a greater use of drama and
determinism. Kuehl demonstrates, in addition, how
determinism figures in Hawkes's method of characterization and discusses the writer's use of characters to
represent ideas or forces and his post-1960's penchant
for psychological characterization. Delving next into
Hawkes's growing preference for first-person narrators, Kuehl finishes by extensively analyzing The Blood
Oranges to illustrate many of his remarks.

594. Kuehl, Linda. "Talk with James Laughlin: New and
    Old Directions." New York Times Book Review,
    February 25, 1973, pp. 46-8. [47]
    In the course of this interview Laughlin has the
opportunity to utter a few statements in praise of
Hawkes's heightened prose or "voice," his manipula-
tion of comedy, and his continued growth from novel
to novel. Says Laughlin, in concluding: "Essentially
Hawkes is just pure 'genius,'..."

595. The Landscape of the Imagination. [Sound Recording]
    British Broadcasting Corporation, 1967. 2 tapes,
    12 in. reels, 15 ips., mono., 60 minutes?
    Broadcast on the Third Programme on June 27,
1967 from 7:30 to 8:30 P.M., this show attempts to
examine the main themes of Hawkes's novels, ascertain
their difficulties, and point out their individual qualities. Hawkes himself reads passages from The Cannibal, The Lime Twig, and Second Skin, while Paul
Meyersberg, Eric Rhode, and Christopher Ricks carry
on the discussion with George MacBeth as moderator.
No scripts of this program are available.

596. LeClair, Thomas (Edmund). "Death and Black Humor."
    Critique (Atlanta) 17, no. 1 (1975), pp. 5-40.

[17, 19-21]

While discussing how characters in selected modern novels react to the fear of death, LeClair chooses Skipper from Hawkes's Second Skin as an example of a character who steadfastly denies the influence of death over his life and cultivates an "innocence" that causes innocent people suffering and leads to their death. He notes, further, that Hawkes manages to treat the relationship of death and innocence with "brutal humor" not only in Second Skin, but also in The Blood Oranges and Death, Sleep & the Traveler.

597.   Le Vot, André. "Kafka Reconstructed, ou le Fantastique de John Hawkes." Recherches anglaises et américaines 6 (1973): 127-41.

Although a comparison of Hawkes's imagination with that of Goya or Kafka would be fruitful, at this time an analysis of the theoretical basis and techniques of Hawkes's creations, which are truly the Waste land of the second half of the twentieth century ("le Waste land de la deuxième moitié du vingtième siècle"), is more important. First of all, avowedly committed to innovation and violence in his works, Hawkes develops the characteristic otherworldliness ("le surnaturel") of his novels in four possible ways, whose effective combination can best be seen in an example from The Lime Twig. This "surnaturel," unlike the classical literary type, destroys linear narration, has a cyclical nature, and is promoted through nearly poetic structuring and the negation of the passage of time.

Also, Hawkes's use of a first-person narrator who causes terrifying events is not only contrary to the traditional use of the narrator in classical fantastic fiction but also to Kafka's use. In addition, Hawkes's aim in creating such fiction is unique: he wishes to expose the causes of terrifying events far more than their effects.

598.   Littlejohn, David. "The Anti-realists." Daedalus 92 (Spring 1963): 250-64. [256-58]

The Cannibal is "the most hallucinatory, the most intense, and in many respects the best" of the works of Hawkes, writer of the purest anti-realism since Kafka. None communicates "revolting, inescapable terror" better than he. Yet while The Cannibal's vision of terror and ugliness are justified by "the monumental terror of the chosen locale," much of the horror of the other novels seems sadistic, and the ugliness and decay overdone. Such unpleasant features are likely to drive away otherwise appreciative readers. On the other hand, there is "no better casebook in the recreation of vivid and effective nightmare" than Hawkes's fiction.

598a. Lopez, Hank. "A Country and Some People I Love; an Interview by Hank Lopez with Katherine Anne Porter." Harper's Magazine, September 1965, pp. 58-68. [68]

In response to some questions concerning her opinion of contemporary writers, Miss Porter reveals that she considers the works of Burroughs, Mailer, and Hawkes to be "wretched stuff ... the sort of revolting upchuck that makes the old or Paris-days Henry Miller's work look like plain, rather tepid, but clean and well-boiled tripe."

599. Louie, Elaine. "Hawkes Seeks the Human in Surrealism; Evokes Sympathy through Detachment." Pembroke Record (Providence, R.I.), May 11, 1962, p. 4.

Ms. Louie's remarks, largely summed up by the article's title, were made on the occasion of Hawkes's receipt of the Guggenheim Fellowship. Her comparatively brief piece also includes quotations from Guerard's introduction to The Cannibal and comments on Hawkes's small, but growing, readership.

600. Lundgren, Caj. "John Hawkes' Mörka Myter" (The Dark Myths of John Hawkes). Svenska Dagbladet (Stockholm), November 5, 1969, p. 4.

Writing this article after interviewing Hawkes, Lundgren introduces the novelist as creator of some of the cruelest, most alarming, and most experimental books on the American literary scene today and notices the surprising contrast between the bright and engaging natures of both Providence and Hawkes and the dark, demonic atmosphere found in Hawkes's novels. He includes descriptions of The Lime Twig and Second Skin and comments in a few places on Hawkes's masterful style and use of hallucinatory effects. In fact, he calls The Cannibal one of the most noteworthy books inspired by World War II, and Second Skin Hawkes's most responsive book. Indicating the novelist's answers to questions about the poetic nature of

his books, the continuation of the first-person narrative, and his readership, Lundgren also adds his own
reflections upon Hawkes's thematic use of evil and
method of developing atmosphere, the novelist's small
audience, and the favorable interaction of authors and
students at universities.

601.   Malin, Irving. New American Gothic.   Crosscurrents
        Modern Critiques.   Carbondale: Southern Illinois
        University Press, 1962, pp. 38-44, 71-5, 99-103,
        124-6, 159-60.
        Beginning and ending his treatment of Hawkes with
general statements about the novelist's work and including in his final remarks a listing of Hawkes's limi-
tations, Malin covers in between certain aspects of
Hawkes's fictions by means of examples from his early
novels.   These aspects are: "the inhuman reflections
of narcissism," furthered by mechanical and animal-
istic images (this is a major Hawkesian theme); the
portrayal of adults as perpetual children and innocent
children conflicting with parents (discussion of this aspect is identical to that found in the next item cited,
No. 602); the image of character "entrapment in private worlds," and the voyage image, involving erratic,
violent, or destructive movement.

602.   _____. Psychoanalysis and American Fiction.
        New York: Dutton, 1965, pp. 271-5.
        In discussing the view of the family discoverable
in new American gothic fiction, Malin states that
Hawkes "seems simply to regard adults as perpetual
children, seeking strong parents."   He draws extended
examples from Charivari, The Cannibal, and The
Goose on the Grave and sees, further, in The Cannibal an implication that "distorted, violent families
parallel (or cause?) crazy love of the fatherland" and
in The Goose on the Grave a portrayal of "the innocent child in conflict with the adult world."

603.   Matthews, Charles. "The Destructive Vision of John
        Hawkes." Critique (Atlanta) 6 (Fall 1963): 38-52.
        Analyzes Hawkes's works from The Cannibal to
The Lime Twig as novels of destruction and desolation,
reflecting the "sense of destruction ... which modern
man feels when confronted with ... all human institu-
tions, ideals and ideologies."   Calls The Cannibal "a
picture of the fragmented, disintegrating modern con-

sciousness," likens The Beetle Leg to a "sick dream
of Hell," discovers in The Goose on the Grave a major Hawkesian theme--"the corruption of succeeding
generations by the preceeding ones," and finds in The
Lime Twig that "oppressive loneliness which is created and maintained by the tedium of the common-
place." In addition, includes comments on the destructive power of religion and ritual in several episodes and on Hawkes's brand of humor, termed "gal-
lows humor."

604.   Nin, Anaïs. "Novel of the Future." Studies in the
Twentieth Century 1 (Spring 1968): 79-108. [89-
92]
            Quotes several lines from Guerard's introduction
to The Cannibal and from Leslie Fiedler's to The
Lime Twig to explain Hawkes's technique, and pays
tribute to the quality of Hawkes's style despite her
dislike of "sadism and violence." In addition, specu-
lates from Guerard's praise of Hawkes that a possible
reason for lack of support for her own work and that
of other female writers is the fact that she and these
other women create studies of love while Hawkes produces much-admired studies of destruction and sadism.

605.   _____ . The Novel of the Future. New York: Mac-
millan, 1968, pp. 176-8.
            A slightly revised, slightly shortened version of
the pages on Hawkes described in the preceding item,
No. 604.

606.   Oberbeck, S. K. "John Hawkes: the Smile Slashed
by a Razor." In Contemporary American Novelists, pp. 193-204. Edited by Harry T. Moore.
Carbondale: Southern Illinois University Press,
1964; reprinted in The Merrill Studies in Second
Skin, pp. 45-52 (No. 537); excerpted in Modern
American Literature, p. 53 (No. 587).
            "Astonishing sympathy, satanic humor [and] cold
detachment" are the terms which best describe Hawkes's
fiction--a fiction evidencing creative energy comparable
to that of such writers as Faulkner or Kafka. Also
found in Hawkes's works are a richness of language
and conception that is neatly summarized with difficulty
and creative settings of great depth and sensitivity
which possess a "particular kind of timeless violence."

Moreover, one experiences each novel like a hallucinatory dream, whose terrifying aftermath cannot be es-
caped even upon waking. Hawkes recreates, as few
other American authors do, "the mixture of pity and
exhilaration in the human condition," which results
from his relentless search into the terrifying truth
about everything.

607.   The Oxford Companion to American Literature, 4th ed.
        S. v. "Hawkes, John."
        A paragraph of short comments on Hawkes's first
five novels, preceded by a few biographical statements
and followed by a general remark on the complex style
and "dense plot structure" of the books.

608.   Palmer, W. F. "Hawkes and The Lime Twig." Brown
        Daily Herald Supplement 4 (February 28, 1961): 12.
        Hawkes, a master of pure prose, eschews "real"
experience in his writing of human terror, love, and
obscenity and lacks popularity because his message is
distasteful. "It is the true and pure starkness, the
unsympathetic and unrelenting judgments of Hawkes'
reality which we most fear..."

609.   Ratner, Marc. "The Constructed Vision: The Fiction
        of John Hawkes." Studi Americani 11 (1965): 345-
        57.
        Illustrated by several examples, initial observa-
tions on the predominance of the imagination in Hawkes's
theory of the novel and in his works are followed by
remarks on the novelist's poetic technique, as well as
on Hawkes's success in reiterating in his novels the
"dominance of history over man's lives and their inabil-
ity to escape their past." Indeed, an extended analysis
of The Cannibal displays Hawkes's "compressed poetic
prose," "vaguely symbolic characterization similar to
the figural realism of Dante," and original view of reality, dependent on his projection of symbols and myths
of the past on the modern world. Specific to The Cannibal, Ratner feels is that here Hawkes makes the
characters "symbolic of the social and political forces
at work in twentieth century Europe."

610.   Romano, John. "Our Best-Known Neglected Novelist."
        Commentary, May 1974, pp. 58-60.
        Though increasing in reputation, Hawkes still baf-
fles the public with the difficulties of his novels or of-

fends them with the violence of his works. Yet he
"toys ably with our capacities for dread" and shows
a mastery of style that is widely praised. Nonetheless, some of his symbolism is timeworn, some uses
of psychology simplistic or inconsistent with his anti-
realistic aims, and some attempts to maintain realistic visceral appeal result in "confusion of aims and
indecisiveness of effect." An old-fashioned experimen-
talist who still "portrays the pain of our dislocation
of our existence," Hawkes has created his best novel
in Second Skin, a work of great conviction and power.

611.   Rovit, Earl. "The Fiction of John Hawkes: an In-
           troductory View." Modern Fiction Studies 10
           (Summer 1964): 150-62; excerpted in Modern
           American Literature, p. 52 (No. 587).
           In investigating Hawkes's ability to create fictions
which "engage, sensitize, paralyze, and release with
a renewed vitality the slumbering energies of the human spirit," Rovit explores the novelist's unique use
of "a single dramatic plot with flashbacks in time and
extensions in space," of narrative focus, and of a
style, termed "dominantly visual kinetic," in which
the reader is compelled to become part of the fiction.
He then delves into thematic bases of Hawkes's works:
the existence of a "there"--a reality which lies beyond
our ability to distort or disturb it, and the relationship of victim and victimizer. In addition, Rovit
looks at the change in Hawkes's concept of his role
as an artist from The Cannibal to The Lime Twig and
talks of Hawkes as a Kierkegaardian humorist and his
work as "a vehicle of life-affirmation."

612.   Scholes, Robert. The Fabulators. New York: Ox-
           ford University Press, 1967, pp. 59-94.
           Presenting Hawkes as a fabulator writing in the
picaresque tradition, Scholes draws on some of the
novelist's comments in his interview with Enck (No.
78) to indicate the relationship of Hawkes's fiction with
that of previous writers. He next provides a more
detailed analysis of these comments which delves into
the questions of plot versus structure, development of
structure by consciousness working on materials liberated from the unconscious, and the role of structure
in giving pleasure to the reader. In the last twenty
pages of this treatment of Hawkes, Scholes looks to
Charivari and The Lime Twig to illustrate Hawkes's

attitude towards cruelty in fiction and to demonstrate
that Hawkes's narrative power relies on the interaction of cruel wit and tenderness. He also suggests
that Hawkes's care for form makes beautiful the horrible materials with which he works.

613. Schott, Webster. "John Hawkes, American Original."
      New York Times Book Review, May 29, 1966, pp.
      4, 24-5.
      Schott declares Hawkes to be "one of the most in-
ventive and evolving--and publically neglected--novel-
ists alive in the United States" and one who offers us
novels containing "visions of life as a terrible illness
endured in a ravaged landscape, hope as a wild collu-
sion of comic circumstances." Disclosing the origins
of Hawkes's early fictions and commenting briefly on
each work, he considers Second Skin (the latest novel
at the time) to be the novelist's triumph and names it
a "beautiful ugly story," much like an elaborate poem,
in which hope is imparted to the order of things.
Schott's final paragraphs praise Hawkes for anticipat-
ing in art our contemporary need to search our souls,
for prophesizing our emotions better than any other
living American writer, and for catching in his astonishing imaginative works "the rhythm of our secret
processes."

614. Seymour-Smith, Martin. Funk & Wagnalls Guide to
      Modern World Literature. New York: Funk &
      Wagnalls, 1973, pp. 144-6.
      Feels that Hawkes is "a genuine experimental
writer," who produces heavily rhetorical, but power-
fully imaginative, works. Sees a similarity between
Djuna Barnes and Hawkes with respect to "the integrity of the peculiar atmosphere" of their work, although judges Hawkes to have superior methods. After a few brief statements about Hawkes's individual
novels, concludes by designating Hawkes as "one of
the leading writers of his generation."

615. Spencer, Sharon. Space, Time and Structure in the
      Modern Novel. New York: New York University
      Press, 1971, pp. 29-32, 82-4, 88-90, passim.
      Scattered references to three of Hawkes's works
indicate a few important features of these novels.
"Subordination of character to a total vision spatially
concerned" is pointed out in The Cannibal; Second

Skin is discussed with respect to several aspects of
its first-person narration; and the roles of Slyter and
Hencher in The Lime Twig are analyzed to show the
"relationship between narrative point of view and structure, and of the role of the reader's reconciling third
perspective."

616. Spiegel, Alan. "A Theory of the Grotesque in South-
      ern Fiction." Georgia Review 26 (Winter 1972):
      426-37 [434]
      A passing mention of Hawkes's works as an ex-
ample of the modern expression of "the Gothic perspective," in which both the subject matter and technique are composed of "the violent, the ugly, and the
distorted."

617. Tanner, Tony. "Necessary Landscapes and Luminous
      Deteriorations." TriQuarterly, no. 20 (Winter
      1971), pp. 145-79; reprinted in his City of Words:
      American Fiction 1950-1970, pp. 202-29. New
      York: Harper & Row, 1971.
      Drawing upon Hawkes's own words about his writ-
ing, Tanner offers one reason for the novelist's use of
fictional landscapes: the pursuit of absolute detachment. He then suggests as an additional reason the
perfect opportunity such landscapes afford to Hawkes
to turn life's "ungainly deteriorations" into "luminous"
ones by means of his stylistic techniques. Tanner explores these "necessary" landscapes in each of Hawkes's
fictions through Second Skin but concentrates most heavily on The Cannibal, The Lime Twig, and Second Skin.
He provides extensive commentary also on such aspects
of Hawkes's work as the parody of Hawkes as a writer
in The Cannibal, the suggestion in The Lime Twig that
"evil is in part summoned up by the dreams of innocence," the many possible meanings of "skin" and
"second skin" in Second Skin, and the portrayal of
Skipper, the narrator of Second Skin.

618. Tisdale, Bob. "The Flesh Made Words." Carleton
      Miscellany 14 (Fall/Winter 1973/74): 104-7; ex-
      cerpted in Contemporary Literary Criticism, p.
      215 (No. 586).
      Ostensibly a review of Busch's book on Hawkes
(No. 570), this piece departs significantly from commenting on Busch's analysis to argue that Hawkes
lacks a "compelling and convincing narrative style."

Tisdale then voices his dislike for experimental novels, if they demonstrate a "loss of narrative moxie."

619. Trachtenberg, Alan. "Barth and Hawkes: Two Fabu-
      lists." Critique (Atlanta) 6 (Fall 1963): 4-18.
      The half dozen pages concerning Hawkes's novels
focus largely on the ways in which these fictions comment on the "world of decay" or the "nightmare of
history" in which we dwell. Discussion of The Cannibal, The Lime Twig, The Goose on the Grave, and
The Owl all serve to illustrate this intent of Hawkes's
works. Both Barth and Hawkes receive commendations
for their treatment of the theme of the "obscurity of
life" in a more personal form than that of the traditional novel, and both are praised for their success in
demonstrating the continued vitality of the novel form.

620. "Which Authors Have Written the Most Distinguished
      Fiction during the Period 1945-65?" Washington
      Post, September 26, 1965, Book Week, pp. 2-3.
      [3]
      The results of a survey which posed the title ques-
tion shows Hawkes in sixteenth place out of a possible
twenty. A few explanatory statements touch upon
Hawkes as "the least known of our important writers"
and note his growing reputation as witnessed by his
near-winning of the National Book Award for 1965.
See No. 60 for a citation to Hawkes's reply to questioning concerning his inclusion on this list, and to
Paul West's statement in defense of his nomination of
Hawkes for the honor.

621. Widner, Kingsley. The Literary Rebel. With a Pref-
      ace by Harry T. Moore. Carbondale: Southern
      Illinois University Press, 1965, p. 164.
      The barest of all bare mentions of Hawkes, in
which the novelist is dubbed a mediocre, unrebellious
writer.

PART VI

MASTERS' THESES AND DOCTORAL
DISSERTATIONS ON HAWKES

622. Armstrong, Thomas William. "The Form of John
      Hawkes' Fiction." Ph.D. dissertation, Univer-
      sity of Illinois at Urbana-Champaign, 1955. Ab-
      stract in Dissertation Abstracts International, 36
      (1975), 2833-A - 2834-A.

623. Atkinson, Michael. "A Phenomenological Approach to
      Experimental Fiction." Ph.D. dissertation, Penn-
      sylvania State University, 1970. Abstract in Dis-
      sertation Abstracts International, 31 (1971),
      4754-A.
      Studies the elements of phenomenology and analyz-
    es Robbe-Grillet's Jealousy, Proust's Swann's Way,
    and Hawkes's The Lime Twig in the light of these ele-
    ments. The discussion of Hawkes's work concentrates
    on "the role of perception in the novel."

624. Blake, Donald David. "Singer of Love: the Fiction
      of John Hawkes." Ph.D. dissertation, State Uni-
      versity of New York at Binghamton, 1974. Ab-
      stract in Dissertation Abstracts International, 35
      (1975), 4501-A.

625. Busch, Frederick. "A John Hawkes Bestiary: Ani-
      mal Imagery in the Novels of John Hawkes."
      Master's Essay, Columbia University, 1967.

626. Eichel, Seymour. "Myth, Ritual and Symbol in the
      Novels of John Hawkes." Ph.D. dissertation,
      New York University, 1972. Abstract in Disser-
      tation Abstracts International, 34 (1973), 3388-A.

627. Fitzgerald, Ellen. "World War II in the American

Novel: Hawkes, Heller, Kosinski, and Vonnegut."
Ph. D. dissertation, University of Notre Dame,
1974. Abstract in Dissertation Abstracts International, 35 (1974), 3736-A - 3737-A.
With respect to Hawkes, examines the surrealistic
techniques of The Cannibal.

628.   Frost, Helen Lucile Pritchard. "A Legacy of Vio-
        lence: John Hawkes' Vision of Culture." Ph. D.
        dissertation, University of Rochester, 1969. Ab-
        stract in Dissertation Abstracts International, 30
        (1970), 3941-A.

629.   Glass, Terrence L. "Myths, Dreams and Reality:
        Cycles of Experience in the Novels of John Hawkes."
        Ph. D. dissertation, Ohio State University, 1973.
        Abstract in Dissertation Abstracts International,
        34 (1974), 5171-A.

630.   Golden, Robert Edward. "Violence and Art in Post-
        war American Literature: a Study of O'Connor,
        Kosinski, Hawkes, and Pynchon." Ph. D. disser-
        tation, University of Rochester, 1972. Abstract
        in Dissertation Abstracts International, 33 (1972),
        311-A.

631.   Green, James Lee. "Nightmare and Dream in John
        Hawkes's Novels." Ph. D. dissertation, University
        of Nevada, Reno, 1971. Abstract in Dissertation
        Abstracts International, 33 (1972), 312-A.

632.   Heath, William Ralph. "John Hawkes: a Critical
        Study." Ph. D. dissertation, Case Western Re-
        serve University, 1971. Abstract in Dissertation
        Abstracts International, 32 (1971), 3305-A.

633.   Heineman, Alan. "Amusing Creations Out of Poison-
        ous Smoke: the Novels of John Hawkes." Ph. D.
        dissertation, Brandeis University, 1974. Abstract
        in Dissertation Abstracts International, 35 (1974),
        3743-A - 3744-A.

634.   Johnson, Joseph James. "The Novels of John Hawkes
        and Julien Gracq: a Comparison." Ph. D. disser-
        tation, Vanderbilt University, 1970. Abstract in
        Dissertation Abstracts International, 31 (1970),
        1280-A.

635.   Leana, Frank C.   "The Power of Language in the
        Novels of John Hawkes."   Ph. D. dissertation,
        University of Rochester, 1974.   Abstract in Dis-
        sertation Abstracts International, 35 (1974),
        2280-A.

636.   LeClair, Thomas Edmund.   "Final Words: Death and
        Comedy in the Fiction of Donleavy, Hawkes,
        Barth, Vonnegut, and Percy."   Ph. D. disserta-
        tion, Duke University, 1972.   Abstract in Disser-
        tation Abstracts International, 33 (1973), 5731-A.

637.   Nelson, Paula Kellner.   "The Function of Figures of
        Speech in Selected Anti-realistic Works."   Ph. D.
        dissertation, New York University, 1972.   Ab-
        stract in Dissertation Abstracts International, 33
        (1972), 1736-A - 1737-A.
        Relates the figures of speech to the structure and
        meaning of Djuna Barnes's Nightwood and Hawkes's
        The Cannibal.

638.   Nelson, Robert McDowell.   "Some Instances of Double
        Vision in Post-War American Fiction: Essays on
        Knowles, Hawkes, and Barth."   Ph. D. disserta-
        tion, Stanford University, 1975.   Abstract in Dis-
        sertation Abstracts International, 36 (1975), 2826-
        A.
        One chapter examines The Lime Twig "in relation
        to the emphatically nightmarish works preceding it and
        the more positive, but also more muted, works follow-
        ing it."

639.   Norwood, Vera L. H.   "Whatever Happened to Natty
        Bumpo?: John Hawkes and the American Tradi-
        tion."   Ph. D. dissertation, University of New
        Mexico, 1973.   Abstract in Dissertation Abstracts
        International, 35 (1974), 1665-A.

640.   Parris, Stephen Anthony.   "An Analysis of First-Per-
        son Narration in the Novels of John Hawkes."
        Master's Essay, University of South Carolina,
        1975.

641.   Scott, Henry Edward.   "The Terrifying Similarity:
        the Themes and Techniques of John Hawkes."
        Ph. D. dissertation, University of Wisconsin,
        1968.   Abstract in Dissertation Abstracts Inter-

national, 29 (1968), 878-A - 879-A.
Explores especially the shaping of form and content in selected novels by the author's philosophical,
psychological, and moral preoccupations.   Chosen for
study from Hawkes's corpus are The Cannibal and
Second Skin.

642.   Slotnick, Linda.   "The Minotaur Within: Varieties of
        Narrative Distortion and Reader Implication in the
        Works of Franz Kafka, John Hawkes, Vladimir
        Nabokov, and Alain Robbe-Grillet."   Ph.D. dis-
        sertation, Stanford University, 1970.   Abstract in
        Dissertation Abstracts International, 31 (1971),
        6071-A - 6072-A.

643.   Smith, Marcus Ayres Joseph.   "The Art and Influence
        of Nathanael West."   Ph.D. dissertation, Univer-
        sity of Wisconsin, 1964.   Abstract in Dissertation
        Abstracts International, 25 (1965), 4155-A - 4156-
        A.
        The seventh chapter investigates West's influence
        on Hawkes and on ten other post-World War II Ameri-
        can novelists.

644.   Tajuddin, Mohammad.   "The Tragicomic Novel: Cam-
        us, Malamud, Hawkes, Bellow."   Ph.D. disserta-
        tion, Indiana University, 1967.   Abstract in Dis-
        sertation Abstracts International, 28 (1968), 2698-
        A - 2699-A.

645.   Weinstein, Sharon Rosenbaum.   "Comedy and Night-
        mare: the Fiction of John Hawkes, Kurt Vonne-
        gut, Jr., Jerzy Kosinski, and Ralph Ellison."
        Ph.D. dissertation, University of Utah, 1971.   Ab-
        stract in Dissertation Abstracts International, 32
        (1971), 3336-A.

646.   Yshamp, Claire E.   "Character and Voice: First-
        person Narrators in Tom Jones, Wuthering
        Heights, and Second Skin."   Ph.D. dissertation,
        Brandeis University, 1972.   Abstract in Disserta-
        tion Abstracts International, 32 (1972), 6948-A.

PART VII

HAWKES BIBLIOGRAPHIES

647. Adelman, Irving and Dworkin, Rita. "Hawkes, John,
      1925- ." In their The Contemporary Novel; a
      Checklist of Critical Literature on the British and
      American Novel since 1945, pp. 250-2. Metuchen,
      N. J. : The Scarecrow Press, 1972.
      A highly selective bibliograpny, composed largely
      of citations to articles and parts of books which ex-
      amine Hawkes's work in general or treat one or more
      of the novels (through Second Skin). Only one review
      and one dissertation are included.

648. Bryer, Jackson R. "Two Bibliographies." Critique
      (Atlanta) 6 (Fall 1963): 86-94. [89-94]
      The earliest comprehensive bibliography on
      Hawkes, which lists the majority of writings by and
      about the novelist through the middle of 1962, includ-
      ing numerous newspaper reviews. [The other bibliog-
      raphy concerns John Barth.]

649. Busch, Frederick. Hawkes: A Guide to His Fictions.
      Syracuse: Syracuse University Press, 1973, pp.
      183-6.
      A bibliographical note in essay form which cites
      several interviews with and critical works by Hawkes,
      Graham's book on Second Skin (No. 537), a few criti-
      cal chapters on and other allusions to Hawkes, numer-
      ous "intelligent reviews" of Hawkes's novels and plays,
      four writings by Guerard on Hawkes, and some "good
      starting-points for further study of Hawkes."

650. Greiner, Donald J. Comic Terror: the Novels of
      John Hawkes. Memphis: Memphis State Univer-
      sity Press, 1973, pp. 249-53.
      This "selected checklist of John Hawkes" offers a

notation of novels, short fiction, plays, and several pieces of criticism by Hawkes, four interviews, Bryer's bibliography (No. 648), and a lengthy list of "criticism of Hawkes and significant reviews." Newspaper reviews are minimal.

651.   [Hawkes, Sophie. John Hawkes Bibliography.] Providence, R. I., 1972. (Typewritten)
        Preceded by a paragraph of biographical data on Hawkes, this bibliography lists all known editions and published works by Hawkes through The Blood Oranges, many English and American reviews, and a dozen or so articles of general criticism on the author's writings. Review and periodical citations do not include page numbers.

652.   Kuehl, John. John Hawkes and the Craft of Conflict. New Brunswick, N. J. : Rutgers University Press, 1975, pp. 191-5.
        Provides a listing of the major writings by Hawkes (with some of the minor), along with the most widely-known interviews and a highly selective catalog of writings about Hawkes.

653.   Nevius, Blake, comp. "Hawkes, John (1925-   )." In The American Novel: Sinclair Lewis to the Present, p. 55. Goldentree Bibliographies in Language and Literature. New York: Appleton-Century-Crofts, 1970.
        A fourteen-item list, chiefly of "biographical and critical essays" on Hawkes, the latest of which was published in 1966.

654.   Olds, Marshall C. "John Hawkes: a Bibliography." Hamilton, N. Y. : Colgate University, 1972. (Typewritten)
        At the date of compilation the most comprehensive bibliography of Hawkes since Bryer's listing.

655.   Plung, Daniel. "John Hawkes: a Selected Bibliography, 1943-1975." Critique (Atlanta) 17, no. 3 (1976): 53-63.
        The latest selective bibliography on Hawkes of considerable length. All types of works by, as well as about, the author are included, with reviews of each major work constituting a substantial part of the bibliography.

SEE ALSO: Nos. 104-5.

NAME INDEX

Included in this index are the names of authors, editors, and translators of the material about Hawkes and his work cited in the bibliography, translators of the novelist's works, directors of productions of his plays, compilers of works containing sections or articles by or about Hawkes, and those few who coauthored or coedited works with John Hawkes.

PERIODICAL INDEX

Included in this index are the names of all periodicals containing works by or about John Hawkes and his writings cited in this bibliography. In a few instances "see also" references have been provided to indicate that the titles connected in this manner are actually title variants of the same periodical.